PHARMACY LAW
SIMPLIFIED

ARIZONA MPJE® STUDY GUIDE

for **2016 - 2017**

BY DAVID A HECKMAN, PHARMD

PHARMACY LAW
SIMPLIFIED

DISCLAIMERS & COPYRIGHT

Pharmacy Law Simplified: Arizona MPJE® Study Guide for 2016 – 2017

ISBN-13: 978-1942682066
ISBN-10: 1942682069

MPJE® is a registered trademark of the National Association of Boards of Pharmacy. This publication is neither affiliated with nor endorsed by the National Association of Boards of Pharmacy.

The author does not assume and hereby disclaims any liability to any party for losses, damages, and/or failures resulting from an error or omission, regardless of cause.

This publication is for informational use only.

This publication is not a substitute for legal advice. For legal advice, consult a legal professional.

This publication does not contain actual exam content.

Copyright © 2016 by David Heckman
All rights reserved. This book is protected by copyright. No portion of this book can be reproduced in any form, including mechanical or electronic reproduction, without express written permission from the author.

Book cover design by Keeling Design & Media, Inc.

Published by Heckman Media.

Printed in the United States of America.

TABLE OF CONTENTS

ARIZONA PHARMACY LAW REVIEW

Arizona State Board of Pharmacy	6
Pharmacist Licensure by Examination	7 – 8
Pharmacist Licensure by Reciprocity	9
Honorary Certificate of Licensure	9
Pharmacy Intern Licensure	10 – 11
Pharmacy Intern Preceptors	12
Intern Training Time	12
Intern Reports to the Board	12
Unique Responsibilities of Pharmacists, Pharmacy Interns, and Graduate Interns	13
Other Unique Responsibilities	14
Pharmacy Technician and Trainee Licensure	15
License Renewal Requirements	16
Reinstating Delinquent Licenses	17
Continuing Education Requirements	18
Licensee Board Notification Requirements	19
Pharmacy, Wholesaler, and Manufacturer Permits	20 – 21
Resident Pharmacy Permits	22
Procedures for Discontinuing a Pharmacy	23
Non-Prescription Drug Permits	24
Resident Drug Manufacturer Permits	25
Resident Drug Wholesaler Permits	26 – 27
Full Service Wholesale Permittees	27
Full Service Wholesaler Transactions	28
Prescription Drug Pedigrees	29
Non-Resident Permits	30
Unethical and Unprofessional Conduct	31 – 32
Unethical Practices	32
Prohibited Acts	32
Adulterated Drugs and Devices	33
Misbranded Drugs and Devices	33
Board Discipline for Pharmacists, Pharmacy Interns, and Graduate Interns	34
Board Discipline for Pharmacy Technicians and Pharmacy Technician Trainees	35
Board Discipline for Pharmacy Permittees	35
Board Hearings	36
Substance Abuse Treatment and Rehabilitation Program	37
Prescription Requirements	38 – 40
Dispensing Prescription Drugs	41
Generic Substitution	42
Prescription Records	43
Returning Drugs and Devices	43
Pharmacy Quality Assurance Programs	44
Patient Counseling Requirements	45
Pharmacist-Administered Immunizations	46 – 47
Implementing, Monitoring, and Modifying Drug Therapy	48
Dispensing Replacement Soft Contact Lenses	48
Declared State of Emergency	49
Prescription Drug Donation Programs	50 – 51
OTC Sale of Methamphetamine Precursors	52
OTC Sale of Dextromethorphan	52
Poisons and Hazardous Substances	53
Controlled Substances: Select Examples	54 – 57
Manufacture, Distribution, and Dispensing of Controlled Substances	58
Controlled Substance Distribution	58
Pharmacy Controlled Substance Inventory Requirements	58
Arizona Controlled Substance Laws	59 – 61
Controlled Substances Prescription Monitoring Program	62
Computer Records	63
Current Good Compounding Practices	64 – 65

PHARMACY LAW
SIMPLIFIED

Imprint Code Requirement for Legend Drugs	66
Community Pharmacy Space and Barrier Requirements	67
Community Pharmacy Personnel and Security Procedures	68
Pharmacy Facility Requirements	69
Pharmacy Equipment Requirements	69
Automated Storage and Distribution Systems	70
Mechanical Storage and Counting Device for Solid Oral Dosage Forms	71
Mechanical Counting Device for Solid Oral Dosage Forms	72
Temporary Pharmacy Facilities or Mobile Pharmacies	72
Shared Services	73
Hospital Pharmacies	74
Hospital Pharmacy Personnel	75
Absence of Pharmacist	76
Hospital Pharmacy Security	77
Hospital Pharmacy Facility Requirements	77
Hospital Pharmacy Equipment	77
Hospital Drug Distribution and Control	78 – 79
Administration of Drugs	79
Investigational Drugs	80
Sterile Compounding	81
Sterile Drug Product Compounding Risk Categories	82
Limited-Service Pharmacies	83
Limited-Service Correctional Pharmacies	84 – 85
Limited-Service Mail-Order Pharmacies	86
Limited-Service Long-Term Care Pharmacy	87
Limited-Service Sterile Pharmaceutical Products Pharmacies	87
Limited-Service Nuclear Pharmacies	88 – 90
Long-Term Care Consultant Pharmacists	91
Provider Pharmacies for Long-Term Care Facilities	92
Long-Term Care Facility Pharmacy Services Emergency Drugs	92 – 93
Long-Term Care Facility Pharmacy Services Emergency Drug Prescription Orders	93
Long-Term Care Facility Pharmacy Services Automated Dispensing Systems	94 – 95
Hospice Inpatient Facilities	96
Assisted Living Facilities	97 – 98
Customized Patient Medication Packages	98
Dietary Supplements	98
Veterinary Drug Distribution	98
Records and Order Forms	99

FEDERAL PHARMACY LAW REVIEW

The Roles of Government Agencies	102
Federal Controlled Substances Act	103 – 107
Drug Addiction Treatment Act of 2000 (DATA 2000)	108
Methadone Dispensing Restrictions	108
DEA Forms	109
Professionals with Prescribing Authority	110
DEA Number Verification	111 – 112
Institutional DEA Numbers	113
Combat Methamphetamine Epidemic Act of 2005 (CMEA)	114
Poison Prevention Packaging Act of 1970 (PPPA)	115
Omnibus Budget Reconciliation Act of 1990 (OBRA '90)	115
Health Insurance Portability & Accountability Act (HIPAA)	116
Generic Substitution and the Orange Book	117
Federal Food, Drug & Cosmetic Act (FD&C Act)	118
Adulterated vs Misbranded	118
Compounding vs Manufacturing	119
Medicaid Tamper-Resistant Prescription Requirement	120
FDA Recalls	121
NDC Numbers	121
Over-the-Counter Drug Labels	122
Restricted Drug Programs	123 – 124
Long-Term Care Facility Pharmacy Services	125

INTRODUCTION

PREPARE THOROUGHLY
The MPJE® is notorious for presenting challenging questions. How can you prepare for this? The answer is simple... thorough preparation. There are no secrets. The more familiar you are with state and federal pharmacy law, the less likely you are to be rattled when faced with a challenging question.

DEFEAT DISTRACTION
As you prepare for this exam, your biggest enemy is distraction. Develop a strategy to avoid distractions now. I recommend studying in a library and leaving your electronic devices at home.

DO NOT TAKE SHORTCUTS
This study guide should be used to review key points in preparation for the Arizona MPJE®. It is not a substitute for Arizona law. Once licensed, you are expected to possess a certain level of professional competence, including knowledge of pharmacy law relevant to your state or jurisdiction. For this reason, it is imperative to review the Arizona Revised Statutes and Arizona Administrative Code as part of your study plan. The Arizona Revised Statutes and Arizona Administrative Code are available on the Arizona State Board of Pharmacy website (https://pharmacy.az.gov).

ARIZONA STATE BOARD OF PHARMACY WEBSITE & NEWSLETTERS
Taking some time to review the other information posted on the Arizona State Board of Pharmacy website may also be helpful when preparing for the MPJE®. Since the website is published directly by the Board of Pharmacy, it can help you better understand how the Board interprets and enforces pharmacy law in Arizona. Board-published newsletters are also helpful for the same reason. The Arizona State Board of Pharmacy Newsletters are available in PDF format at the NABP website (www.NABP.net). For a direct link, visit https://pharmacy.az.gov and look for "Newsletters" under the heading "News & Events."

ARIZONA STATE BOARD OF PHARMACY
ARS § 32-1902

COMPOSITION OF THE ARIZONA STATE BOARD OF PHARMACY

6 Pharmacists*   1 Pharmacy Technician   2 Public Members

*At least 1 pharmacist employed by a licensed hospital & at least 1 pharmacist employed by a community pharmacy. Also, must be practicing pharmacists.

- ✓ Board members are appointed by the GOVERNOR.

BOARD MEMBER ELIGIBILITY REQUIREMENTS

PHARMACIST MEMBERS: Must have 10 years of experience (minimum) practicing pharmacy in any state, and in the most recent 5 years he/she must have been a resident and a licensed pharmacist in Arizona.

PHARMACY TECHNICIAN MEMBER: Must have 5 years of experience (minimum) in any state, and in the most recent 5 years he/she must have been a resident and a licensed pharmacy technician in Arizona.

PUBLIC MEMBERS: Must have been a resident of Arizona for the most recent 5 years preceding the date of appointment.

BOARD MEMBER TERM LENGTHS

PHARMACIST MEMBERS: Must serve for 5 years.

PHARMACY TECHNICIAN MEMBERS: Must serve for 5 years.

PUBLIC MEMBERS: May serve for up to 5 years, but subject to removal by the Governor. Also, public members are required to submit an annual written report to the Governor.

RECOMMENDATIONS TO THE GOVERNOR

The Executive Director of the Pharmacy Association of Arizona may annually submit a list of at least seven (7) names of association members nominated to fill any soon-to-be vacant pharmacist and/or pharmacy technician seat(s) on the Board. These are merely recommendations. The Governor is not required to select appointees from this list.

PHARMACY LAW
SIMPLIFIED

PHARMACIST LICENSURE BY EXAMINATION
R4-23-201 & ARS § 32-1922

- ✓ Before practicing as a pharmacist in Arizona, one must obtain a valid pharmacist license.

- ✓ Before a pharmacist can work in a pharmacy, the pharmacist-in-charge or permittee must verify that the pharmacist holds a current license.

- ✓ A pharmacist license can be obtained either by examination or by reciprocity.

PHARMACIST LICENSE BY EXAMINATION ELIGIBILITY REQUIREMENTS
- ✓ Good moral character.
- ✓ Graduate from a school or college of pharmacy approved by the Board or the ACPE. *
- ✓ Complete the required practical experience under the supervision of a licensed pharmacist and provide affidavits to serve as proof.
- ✓ Pass the NAPLEX® and the Arizona MPJE®.

*To sit for the NAPLEX® and MPJE®, foreign pharmacy graduates must first pass a Board-approved preliminary equivalency exam that includes the testing of English proficiency in addition to academic subjects related to pharmacy AND complete at least 1500 hours of intern training. If the applicant fails the preliminary exam, he/she must provide the Board with written proof that Board-approved remedial academic work was completed to correct deficiencies before retaking the exam.

PHARMACIST LICENSE BY EXAMINATION APPLICATION PROCEDURE

Applicant fills out and sends an application to the Board.

⇩

The Board receives the application.

⇩

Within 60 days, the Board must complete an "administrative completeness review" and provide the applicant with written notice of completeness or incompleteness.

⇩

If the Board does not provide a written notice within 60 days after receiving the application, the application is deemed "complete." If the Board provides a written notice of incompleteness within 60 days, then the applicant must submit all missing information within 90 days of receiving the notice. If this is not possible, the applicant can submit a written request for an extension postmarked no later than 90 days after receiving the notice of incompleteness. A 30-day extension may be granted at the discretion of the Board.

⇩

The Board must complete a "substantive review" of the applicant's qualifications within 120 days after the administrative completeness review is complete.

⇩ ⇩

Applicants deemed ELIGIBLE to take the NAPLEX® and MPJE® will receive an "authorization to test" (ATT) from the NABP, which is valid for 12 months from the date the Board received the initial application.	Applicants deemed INELIGIBLE to take the NAPLEX® and MPJE® will receive written notice of denial from the Board.

TOTAL TIME REQUIRED TO OBTAIN PHARMACIST LICENSE BY EXAMINATION
60 days for administrative completeness review + 120 days for substantive review* = 180 days
* Plus up to 90 days for additional documentation if the initial application is incomplete.

NAPLEX® & MPJE®

✓ A scaled score of at least 75 is required to pass both the NAPLEX® and the MPJE®.

✓ If an applicant fails the NAPLEX® or MPJE® three (3) times, he/she must petition and obtain Board approval prior to retaking.

✓ For license by examination applicants, the Board considers passing scores on the NAPLEX® and MPJE® to be valid for 24 months. If an application is incomplete at the time the score(s) expire, the applicant will be required to retake the examination(s).

NAPLEX® SCORE TRANSFER

NAPLEX® examinees who pass the exam in one state/jurisdiction can have their NAPLEX® score transferred to other states/jurisdictions via the National Association of Boards of Pharmacy (NABP). Score transfer allows the examinee to obtain a license by examination in more than one (1) state. According to the NABP, a score transfer request may be submitted up to 90 days after sitting for the NAPLEX®.

Note: After the Arizona Board of Pharmacy receives a score transfer, the applicant must complete an application for licensure by examination within 12 months.

PHARMACIST LICENSURE BY RECIPROCITY
R4-23-203 & ARS § 32-1922

A pharmacist may obtain an Arizona pharmacist license by reciprocity if he/she possesses a license by examination in good standing for at least one year in a state/jurisdiction that provides reciprocity to Arizona-licensed pharmacists.

PHARMACIST LICENSE BY RECIPROCITY ELIGIBILITY REQUIREMENTS
- ✓ Good moral character.
- ✓ Complete the required secondary and professional education/training.
- ✓ Possess a LICENSE BY EXAMINATION in good standing from another US state/jurisdiction for at least one (1) year with a minimum of 400 hours of pharmacist experience over the past calendar year.
  OR
- ✓ Complete intern training that meets the LICENSE BY EXAMINATION requirements in the year immediately prior to the date of application AND complete a minimum of 400 hours of graduate internship experience in a Board-approved intern training site while licensed as an Arizona graduate intern.
- ✓ Submit proof of a passing score on the NABPLEX® or NAPLEX® (If examined after June 1, 1979).
- ✓ Pass the Arizona MPJE®.
  - ⇨ Applicants must register with the NABP before sitting for the Arizona MPJE®.

Note: An applicant for pharmacist licensure by reciprocity must also prove that their licenses from other states/jurisdictions have not been suspended, revoked, or restricted for reasons other than non-renewal or failure to obtain required continuing education.

HONORARY CERTIFICATE OF LICENSURE
ARS § 32-1922

Pharmacists licensed in Arizona for 50 years will receive an honorary pharmacist license. These licensees must follow the same rules as other licensed pharmacists (e.g. same CE requirements); however, they are not required to pay license renewal fees.

⇩

NO RENEWAL FEES

PHARMACY INTERN LICENSURE

ARS § 32-1923, R4-23-301, & R4-23-302

All interns must obtain a license from the Board prior to working as an intern, and certificates of licensure must be kept in the practice site (i.e. pharmacy) for Board inspection or public review.

Prior to allowing an employee to act as a pharmacy intern, the pharmacist-in-charge or pharmacy permittee must verify that the individual holds an active intern license. This can be done at the Arizona State Board of Pharmacy website.

PHARMACY INTERN LICENSE ELIGIBILITY REQUIREMENTS

To qualify for a PHARMACY INTERN license, an applicant must be enrolled and in good standing at a Board-approved school or college of pharmacy AND provide one (1) of the following: *
- An official transcript.
- A letter from the dean.
- A letter from the registrar.

GRADUATE INTERN LICENSE ELIGIBILITY REQUIREMENTS

To qualify for a GRADUATE INTERN license, an applicant must be a graduate of a Board-approved school or college of pharmacy, submit an application for pharmacist licensure by examination or reciprocity (or receive order from the Board to complete intern training), AND provide one (1) of the following: *
- Final transcripts that indicate the date of graduation.
- A letter from the dean as proof of graduation.
- A letter from the registrar as proof of graduation.

* Documentation requirements as outlined on the application from the AZ Board of Pharmacy website as of March 2016.

Note: According to information at the Arizona Board of Pharmacy website, licensed pharmacy interns should not apply for a separate graduate intern license after graduation. The graduate intern license is reserved for pharmacists who are required by the Board to complete intern hours.

FOREIGN PHARMACY GRADUATES

When the pharmacy intern license applicant is a person who has graduated from a college/school of pharmacy that is NOT Board-approved (e.g. foreign graduates), the applicant must provide a notarized copy of his/her Foreign Pharmacy Graduate Examination Committee (FPGEC) certificate to obtain an intern license.

OPEN VS PENDING STATUS

If an intern applicant receives a license number with an "OPEN" status, he/she can begin employment as an intern immediately (that is… prior to receiving the certificate of licensure). On the other hand, when an intern applicant receives a license number with a "PENDING" status, this means the applicant CANNOT begin working prior to receiving the certificate of licensure.

PHARMACY INTERN TRAINING REQUIREMENTS
The purpose of intern training is to obtain practical experience in the practice of pharmacy prior to becoming a licensed pharmacist.

PHARMACY INTERNS MUST RECEIVE INSTRUCTION IN THE FOLLOWING AREAS DURING AN INTERNSHIP:
- ✓ Manufacturing.
- ✓ Wholesaling.
- ✓ Dispensing.
- ✓ Compounding.
- ✓ Clinical pharmacy.
- ✓ Providing drug information.
- ✓ Maintaining records and creating reports required by state and federal laws.
- ✓ Other experiences necessary to practice the profession of pharmacy.

INTERN TRAINING SITE REQUIREMENTS
INTERN TRAINING SITES MUST BE…
Permitted by the Arizona Board of Pharmacy and employ a preceptor who supervises the intern.
OR
Non-pharmacy training sites* that perform pharmacy-related activities (may or may not be established and monitored by a college/school of pharmacy).

Referred to as "alternative training sites."

BOARD NOTIFICATION RULES
Intern training obtained through a Board-approved college/school of pharmacy experiential training program must be reported to the Board by the college/school; however, training obtained outside of a Board-approved college/school of pharmacy experiential training program must be reported by the intern. The intern must notify the Board within 10 days of the following:
- ✓ Initiating employment.
- ✓ Terminating employment.
- ✓ Changing training sites.

OTHER KEY POINTS
- ✓ If an intern stops attending pharmacy school/college classes, he/she must immediately stop working as an intern and surrender his/her intern license to the Board within 30 days after last attending class.

- ✓ Interns must complete pharmacy school within six (6) years from the date of initial licensure. After six (6) years, re-licensure is only possible with approval from the Board.

- ✓ The Board will grant credit for intern hours obtained outside of Arizona if the intern training requirements meet Arizona's minimum requirements.

ACCORDING TO ARS § 32-1922, A PHARMACIST WHO HAS NOT PRACTICED PHARMACY FOR MORE THAN ONE (1) YEAR MAY BE REQUIRED TO COMPLETE UP TO 400 HOURS OF INTERNSHIP PRIOR TO RESUMING ACTIVE PRACTICE.

PHARMACY INTERN PRECEPTORS
R4-23-302

ELIGIBILITY REQUIREMENTS
To be a preceptor for pharmacy interns, a pharmacist must:
1) Hold a current unrestricted pharmacist license,
2) Have at least one (1) year of experience actively practicing as a pharmacist, AND
3) Hold a faculty position in a Board-approved college/school of pharmacy experiential training program OR obtain Board-approval to act as a preceptor.

Note: If previously found guilty of violating pharmacy law, unprofessional conduct, etc., there must be an agreement that restricts the preceptor's pharmacist license to the satisfaction of the Board

PHARMACIST-TO-INTERN RATIO LIMIT
One (1) pharmacist may supervise up to two (2) interns in a calendar quarter. *

Note: Board approval must be obtained to exceed this ratio. The Board will consider space limitations and potential effect on public safety when deciding whether or not to approve or deny requests to exceed this ratio.

* This limit applies only in community pharmacy and limited-service pharmacy settings. There is no ratio limit in practice settings directed by a Board-approved school/college of pharmacy experiential training program.

PRECEPTOR RESPONSIBILITIES
- ✓ Teach and mentor the intern.
- ✓ Thoroughly review pharmacy policies and procedures with the intern.
- ✓ Take responsibility for the actions of the intern.
- ✓ Provide the intern with opportunities for skill development and timely feedback on progress.

INTERN TRAINING TIME
R4-23-303

- ✓ Minimum time spent in internship training to qualify for pharmacist licensure: 1,500 hours.
- ✓ No more than 500 hours may be obtained at an alternative training site (non-pharmacy training site).
- ✓ An intern must hold a valid pharmacy intern license and obtain all hours through the experiential training program of a Board-approved pharmacy school/college.

INTERN REPORTS TO THE BOARD
R4-23-304

- ✓ Interns must notify the Board within 10 days of a change of address OR change of employer.
- ✓ After graduating from a Board-approved pharmacy college/school, but before sitting for the NAPLEX® or MPJE®, interns must ensure their college/school experiential program director provides the Board with an intern training report.

UNIQUE RESPONSIBILITIES OF PHARMACISTS, PHARMACY INTERNS, AND GRADUATE INTERNS

R4-23-402

- ✓ Receive oral prescription orders.
  - ⇨ Must be reduced to writing and initialed by the pharmacist or intern.
  - ⇨ Must also record the name of the person who orally communicated the prescription order.
- ✓ Take responsibility for obtaining the information for a patient's profile.
  - ⇨ Name, address, phone number, DOB or age, gender, current disease states, known drug allergies and drug reactions, and complete list of current medications and medical devices (if possible).
- ✓ Take responsibility for recording drug therapy comments in the patient profile.
- ✓ Verify the legality and feasibility of dispensing a drug.
  - ⇨ This requires professional judgement and knowledge of the pertinent law, rules and regulations.
  - ⇨ Factors to consider include the patient's allergies, potential drug interactions/incompatibilities, unusual quantities of a controlled substance, the presence and validity of the prescriber's signature, and the frequency of refills.
- ✓ Verify that the dose of a prescription is within proper dosage ranges/limits.
- ✓ Interpret prescriptions and exercise professional judgement to decide whether or not to dispense a drug.
- ✓ Prepare and package medication to dispense (e.g. compounding).
- ✓ Pre-package drugs or supervise the pre-packaging of drugs by pharmacy technicians or trainees.
- ✓ Check prescription order entry data (e.g. confirm correct patient, correct drug/dose, correct instructions).
- ✓ Perform and document a final accuracy check on filled prescriptions.
- ✓ Record the serial number ("Rx number") and the date a drug is dispensed on the original prescription order.
- ✓ Obtain permission to refill a prescription when necessary, and record the date dispensed, quantity dispensed, and name of the authorizing agent.
- ✓ When prescriptions are faxed or sent electronically, print them or reduce them to writing.
- ✓ Verify that filled prescriptions are sold to the correct patient or the authorized agent of the correct patient.
- ✓ Record the name or initials of the pharmacist or intern who originally dispenses a prescription.
- ✓ Record the name or initials of the pharmacist or intern who dispenses a refill.
- ✓ Provide patient counseling.

IDENTIFICATION BADGE REQUIREMENT

Pharmacists and interns (both pharmacy interns and graduate interns) must wear an ID badge that indicates name and position/title while in duty.

OTHER UNIQUE RESPONSIBILITIES
ARS § 32-1961, ARS § 32-1963, & R4-23-608

THE PHARMACIST
Only a pharmacist or intern under direct supervision of a pharmacist can dispense, compound, or sell drugs. *
* Exceptions are detailed in ARS § 32-1921 (e.g. dispensing by a registered nurse practitioner or physician, non-prescription drugs sold at retail, drugs sold by manufacturers and wholesalers).

A pharmacist must be in active personal charge to open, advertise, or conduct a pharmacy, and to use or display titles or symbols such as "drugs, drugstore, drug shop, pharmacy, apothecary."

Pharmacists have authority to make decisions involving pharmacy ethics and interpretation of laws regarding pharmacy practice or drug/device distribution. Pharmacy owners and managers cannot overrule a pharmacist in these matters.

THE PROPRIETOR, MANAGER AND PHARMACIST-IN-CHARGE
The proprietor, manager, and pharmacist-in-charge are responsible for the quality of drugs and devices sold by a pharmacy, except those sold in original packages from the manufacturer.

The proprietor, manager, or pharmacist-in-charge must be able to provide invoices, stock transfer documents, merchandise return memos, and other documentation related to the acquisition or disposal of Rx-only and controlled substance medications within 4 working days of a request by the Board.

The pharmacy owner and manager are responsible for ensuring all pharmacy personnel comply with laws/rules.

PHARMACY LAW
SIMPLIFIED

PHARMACY TECHNICIAN AND TRAINEE LICENSURE
ARS § 32-1923.01, R4-23-1101, R4-23-1102, R4-23-1103, & R4-23-1104

ALL PHARMACY TECHNICIANS and PHARMACY TECHNICIAN TRAINEES must obtain a license from the Board prior to working in a pharmacy, and certificates of licensure must be kept in the practice site (i.e. pharmacy) for Board inspection or public review.

Prior to allowing an employee to act as a pharmacy technician or pharmacy technician trainee, the pharmacist-in-charge or pharmacy permittee must verify that the individual holds an active pharmacy technician or pharmacy technician trainee license. This can be done at the board of pharmacy website.

PHARMACY TECHNICIAN LICENSE ELIGIBILITY REQUIREMENTS
An applicant must be 18 years of age or older AND possess or complete each of the following:
- ✓ Good moral character.
- ✓ High school diploma or GED.
- ✓ Pharmacy technician training program.
- ✓ Pass the PTCB exam. *

* Or other Board-approved pharmacy technician exam.

PHARMACY TECHNICIAN TRAINEE LICENSE ELIGIBILITY REQUIREMENTS
An applicant must be 18 years of age or older AND possess each of the following:
- ✓ Good moral character.
- ✓ High school diploma or GED.

A PHARMACY TECHNICIAN TRAINEE LICENSE IS VALID FOR 24 MONTHS
If a pharmacy technician trainee does not complete the required training program and pass the PTCB exam (or other Board-approved exam) within 24 months of the license issue date, the license expires WITHOUT eligibility for renewal; however, upon special request, the Board MAY (on a one-time basis) allow a person to reapply for a pharmacy technician trainee license after the license expires.

OPEN VS PENDING STATUS
If a pharmacy technician or pharmacy technician trainee license applicant receives a license number with an "OPEN" status, he/she can begin employment as a pharmacy technician immediately (that is… prior to receiving the certificate of licensure). On the other hand, if an applicant receives a license number with a "PENDING" status, this means the applicant CANNOT begin working prior to receiving the certificate of licensure.

PHARMACY TECHNICIAN AND PHARMACY TECHNICIAN TRAINEE JOB DUTIES
- ✓ Record the serial number and date dispensed on the original prescription.
- ✓ Request or accept verbal or electronic refill authorizations from a practitioner or a practitioner's agent (e.g. secretary, nurse).
- ✓ Record information in the refill record or patient profile.
- ✓ Type and affix prescription labels.
- ✓ Reconstitute prescription medications (e.g. amoxicillin oral suspension).
- ✓ Retrieve, measure, count, pour, and/or package drugs for dispensing.
- ✓ Pre-package drug products.

Note: All duties must be completed under the supervision of a licensed pharmacist.

PHARMACY TECHNICIAN COMPOUNDING
Only pharmacy technicians who have completed a pharmacy technician drug compounding training program may assist the pharmacist in compounding prescriptions and sterile or non-sterile pharmaceuticals. Pharmacy technician trainees are not permitted to assist in compounding.

LICENSE RENEWAL REQUIREMENTS

ARS § 32-1925, R4-23-1102, & ARS § 32-1933

- ✓ Licenses for pharmacists and pharmacy technicians must be renewed biennially (every 2 years).
  - ✓ Intern and pharmacy technician trainee licenses are not eligible for renewal.

To renew, the licensee must do each of the following:
- ☐ Complete the "Application for License Renewal."
- ☐ Pay the renewal fee.
- ☐ Fulfill the continuing education requirement.

ASSIGNMENT OF LICENSE RENEWAL DATE

- ✓ License numbers ending with an ODD NUMBER must be renewed by November 1st of each odd-numbered year (e.g. 2017, 2019, 2021).

- ✓ License numbers ending with an EVEN NUMBER must be renewed by November 1st of each even-numbered year (e.g. 2018, 2020, 2022).

- ✓ Applications for license renewal are not accepted more than 60 days before the license expiration date.

FAILURE TO RENEW LICENSE

Failure to renew on or before November 1st of the assigned year results in a suspension of the license. The suspension will be vacated once all past due fees and penalties are paid.

PRORATED RENEWAL FEES FOR NEW LICENSEES

Fees for new pharmacist and pharmacy technician licenses are prorated based on the number of full calendar months remaining until the first renewal date.

DISPLAY OF CURRENT RENEWAL LICENSE

The current renewal license for each licensee must be maintained in the licensee's practice site for Board inspection or review by the public. If the licensee practices/works in more than one location, a duplicate of the current renewal license must be maintained in the licensee's other practice sites. Duplicates can be obtained from the Board for a fee.

REINSTATING DELINQUENT LICENSES
ARS § 32-1925, R4-23-1101, & R4-23-201

REINSTATING AN ARIZONA PHARMACY TECHNICIAN LICENSE
Requirements to reinstate an Arizona pharmacy technician license that has been delinquent for ≥ 5 years:
1) Pay all delinquent annual renewal & penalty fees.
2) Appear before the Board to demonstrate fitness to be a licensed as a pharmacy technician. *
   * Per R4-23-1101, pharmacy technicians can prove fitness for licensure by:
   ✓ Providing proof of current licensure in another state/jurisdiction AND proof of employment during the previous 12 months.
   OR
   ✓ Passing a Board-approved pharmacy technician exam AND completing 20 hours of CE, including two (2) hours on the topic of pharmacy law.

REINSTATING AN ARIZONA PHARMACIST LICENSE
Requirements to reinstate an Arizona pharmacist license that has been delinquent for ≥ 5 years while practicing in another state/jurisdiction:
1) Pass the Arizona MPJE®.
2) Pay all delinquent annual renewal fees and penalties.

Requirements to reinstate an Arizona pharmacist license that has been delinquent for ≥ 5 years pharmacist WITHOUT practicing in another state/jurisdiction in the past 12 months:
3) Pass the Arizona MPJE®.
4) Pay all delinquent annual renewal & penalty fees.
5) Appear before the Board to demonstrate fitness to be licensed as a pharmacist.

CONTINUING EDUCATION REQUIREMENTS
R4-23-1106, R4-23-204, & ARS § 32-1937

Pharmacists and pharmacy technicians must fulfill the continuing education (CE) requirements as outlined below. All CE must be from a Board-approved provider.

PHARMACY TECHNICIANS [R4-23-1106]

✓ Pharmacy technicians must obtain 20 credit hours (2.0 CEUs) of CE every two (2) years including at least 2 credit hours (0.2 CEUs) on the topic of pharmacy law.

✓ Pharmacy technicians licensed for less than 24 months before the first renewal date must complete an amount of CE equal to 0.83 hours multiplied by the number of months between the date of initial licensure and the assigned renewal date.

PHARMACISTS [R4-23-204]

✓ Pharmacists must obtain 30 credit hours (3.0 CEUs) of CE every two (2) years including at least 3 credit hours (0.3 CEUs) on the topic of pharmacy law.

✓ Pharmacists licensed for less than 24 months before the first renewal date must complete an amount of CE equal to 1.25 hours multiplied by the number of months between the date of initial licensure and the assigned renewal date.

✓ Only CE obtained in the two (2) years immediately preceding the renewal date can be used to fulfill the CE requirement for license renewal.

✓ CE obtained in excess of 30 credit hours CANNOT be applied to the next renewal period.

✓ A pharmacist or pharmacy technician who teaches/presents a pharmacy CE course may receive credit for taking the course if he/she follows the same attendance procedures as the audience.

✓ A pharmacist or pharmacy technician cannot claim CE credit for teaching pharmacy courses that are not CE courses.

CONTINUING EDUCATION RECORDKEEPING & REPORTING REQUIREMENTS

✓ Pharmacists and pharmacy technicians must maintain CE statements of credit and/or certificates of completion for five (5) years.

✓ Pharmacists and pharmacy technicians must attest to the number of CE credits earned each biennial (2-year) renewal period on the license renewal form.

✓ If the Board requests proof of compliance with CE requirements, the pharmacist or pharmacy technician must submit proof of CE participation within 20 days.

✓ Failure to complete, record, or report CE may result in license revocation, suspension, or probation.

EXCEPTIONS TO THE CE REQUIREMENT

The CE requirement does not apply the year a licensee graduates from an accredited school/college of pharmacy. For all others, the Board may make an exception to the CE requirement based on a written request for an exception due to an emergency, hardship case, or for good cause. If the Board grants an exception, the pharmacist must pass a Board-approved exam to obtain the renewal.

LICENSEE BOARD NOTIFICATION REQUIREMENTS
ARS § 32-1926, ARS § 32-1926.01, R4-23-405, & R4-23-608

CHANGE OF HOME ADDRESS OR EMPLOYER
ALL LICENSEES (i.e. pharmacists, pharmacy interns, graduate interns, pharmacy technicians, and pharmacy technician trainees) must notify the Executive Director of the Board WITHIN 10 DAYS after a change of home address or employer. Notification must include the new home address and/or the identity of the new employer.

EXCEPTION: A pharmacist-in-charge must notify the Board "immediately" (i.e. within 24 hours) by mail, fax, or e-mail whenever initiating or terminating his/her role as the pharmacist-in-charge.

CHANGE IN RESIDENCY STATUS
Changes in a licensee's residency status (per the US Immigration & Naturalization Service) must also be reported to the Executive Director of the Board. If residency status ceases to be authorized, the licensee must notify the Executive Director of the Board that he/she voluntarily terminates his/her license.

PHARMACY, WHOLESALER, AND MANUFACTURER PERMITS

ARS § 32-1929, ARS § 32-1930, ARS § 32-1931, ARS § 32-1933, R4-23-601, R4-23-604, & R4-23-605

- ✓ Any entity that manufactures, stocks, compounds, dispenses, handles, and/or sells drugs MUST apply for a permit from the Board before engaging in activity. This includes pharmacies, manufacturers, and wholesalers.

- ✓ Each entity must register with the Board biennially (once every two (2) years).

- ✓ For entities with more than one (1) location, a separate permit must be obtained for each location where drugs are handled (e.g. manufactured, distributed, compounded, dispensed, sold).

- ✓ Pharmacies, drug manufacturers, and wholesalers located outside of Arizona must also obtain a non-resident permit to dispense, sell, transfer, or distribute drugs into Arizona.

TYPES OF PERMITS
- ✓ Pharmacy permit.
- ✓ Limited-service pharmacy permit.
- ✓ Full service wholesale drug permit.
- ✓ Non-prescription wholesale drug permit.
    - o Permittee stocks ≤ 30 drugs ⇨ CATEGORY I RETAILER
    - o Permittee stocks > 30 drugs ⇨ CATEGORY II RETAILER
- ✓ Drug manufacturer's permit.
- ✓ Drug packager permit.
- ✓ Drug re-packager permit.
- ✓ Compressed medical gas distributor permit.
- ✓ Durable medical equipment and compressed medical gas supplier permit.

Note: All permits are non-transferable.

PRACTITIONER KICKBACKS AND REBATES ARE PROHIBITED

A pharmacy's permit will be denied or revoked if said pharmacy directly or indirectly compensates a medical practitioner (i.e. provides some type of kickback or rebate) for writing prescriptions.

- ✓ A permit must be conspicuously displayed in the location to which it is registered.

- ✓ All entities are prohibited from selling or offering to sell any product that has been damaged by water, fire, or from human or animal consumption or use. [R4-23-601]

PERMIT RENEWALS

✓ Permits ending with an even number must be renewed on or before November 1st of each even-numbered year (e.g. 2018, 2020, 2022).

✓ Permits ending with an odd number must be renewed on or before November 1st of each odd-numbered year (e.g. 2017, 2019, 2021).

✓ Renewal involves the filing of a renewal application and the payment of a renewal fee.

✓ Permits not renewed by November 1st of the assigned year will be suspended.

✓ The suspension will be lifted after the permittee pays all related penalties and past due fees.

✓ As with new licenses, the fees for new permits will be prorated based on the number of full months remaining between the issuance of the permit and the first renewal date.

RECORDKEEPING REQUIREMENTS

✓ When a business manufactures, re-packages, or re-labels a product*, the date of manufacturing, re-packaging, or re-labeling must be recorded and kept on file for at least three (3) years.

✓ Whenever a product* is received, sold, delivered, or disposed of, the identity of the product, the identity of the person on each end of the transaction, and the date of the transaction must be recorded and kept on file for at least three (3) years.

* Controlled substance, Rx-only drug or device, non-prescription drug, precursor or regulated chemical.

✓ For full-service or non-prescription drug wholesalers, these records must be made available for Board inspection during normal business hours. Records stored at a central (i.e. off-site) location, must be made available within two (2) business days.

✓ Drug manufacturer permittees must maintain records regarding production, process control, labeling, packaging, quality control, distribution, and complaints. These records and the records required by CGMP (21 CFR 210 – 211) must be kept for at least two (2) years after a drug is distributed or one (1) year after the expiration date of the product, whichever is longer.

✓ Drug manufacturer records must be made available within 48 hours of a request by the Board.

✓ Entities that manufacture radiopharmaceuticals are also required to hold an Arizona Radiation Regulatory Agency Radioactive Materials License and comply with the requirements of the Arizona Radiation Regulatory Agency, the United States Nuclear Regulatory Commission, and the FDA.

RESIDENT PHARMACY PERMITS
R4-23-606

The requirements outlined in this section apply to community, hospital, and limited-service pharmacies.

OPERATION OF A PHARMACY WITHOUT A PERMIT IS PROHIBITED.

To obtain a pharmacy permit, an applicant must submit:
- ✓ Completed application with application fee.
- ✓ Documentation showing compliance with local zoning laws (if required by the Board).
- ✓ Floor plan (including size and security) of the proposed pharmacy area.
- ✓ Copy of the lease for the building/space (if applicable).
- ✓ Disclosure statement regarding whether or not a medical practitioner will receive direct or indirect compensation from the pharmacy.

Before a pharmacy permit can be issued, the Board must:
- ✓ Approve the permit application.
- ✓ Receive a satisfactory inspection report from a Board compliance officer.

Note: The Board may also interview the applicant and the pharmacist-in-charge.

Pharmacy permittees must notify the Board within ten (10) days of a change in:
- ✓ Type of pharmacy operated.
- ✓ Phone number.
- ✓ Fax number.
- ✓ E-mail address.
- ✓ Mailing address.
- ✓ Name of business.
- ✓ Staff pharmacist.

A pharmacy permittee must notify the Board "immediately" (i.e. within 24 hours) of a change (or a pending change) in the person acting as the pharmacist-in-charge.

If non-prescription drugs are sold while the pharmacy area is closed, the permittee must also hold a current non-prescription drug permit.

For changes in ownership involving stock ownership of 30% or more, the prospective owner must submit a new application (with application fee) at least 14 days prior to the change in ownership.

At least 30 days before a pharmacy is relocated or remodeled, the pharmacy permittee must submit a new application to the Board.

PROCEDURES FOR DISCONTINUING A PHARMACY

ARS § 32-1930 & R4-23-613

- ✓ The pharmacy permittee or pharmacist-in-charge must provide written notice to the Board and the DEA at least 14 days before discontinuing a pharmacy business.

- ✓ The written notice should include a specific proposed date for discontinuing the business.

- ✓ The notice must indicate the location to which the drugs, transaction records, prescription files, and patient profiles will be sold, kept, or transferred.

- ✓ Drug and medical device purchase and disbursement records must be kept for at least three (3) years after the date the business is discontinued.

- ✓ Prescription records and patient profiles must be kept for at least seven (7) years from the date the last original or refill prescription was dispensed.

- ✓ After closing, all pharmacy signs and symbols should be removed from inside and outside the building.

- ✓ All state permits and certificates must be returned to the Board of Pharmacy.

- ✓ The DEA registration certificate and all unused DEA 222 forms must be returned to the DEA.

- ✓ When transferring controlled substances upon discontinuation of a pharmacy business, inventory must be taken and a copy of the inventory must accompany the controlled substances being transferred. The original inventory document must be kept for at least three (3) years from the date the business was discontinued. Also, a DEA Form 222 must be used to document the transfer of C-II controlled substances.

PHARMACY LAW SIMPLIFIED

NON-PRESCRIPTION DRUG PERMITS
R4-23-603

To sell or distribute non-prescription drugs, non-pharmacy retailers such as grocery stores, convenience stores, health food stores, swap-meet vendors, and vending machines* must possess a current Board-issued permit.
⇨ Medical practitioners are exempt from this requirement.

PRODUCTS MUST REMAIN IN MANUFACTURER'S ORIGINAL PACKAGING

Non-prescription drug permittees can only sell drugs in the manufacturer's original packaging.

All drugs stocked, sold, or offered for sale must be kept clean, protected from deteriorating factors (e.g. sunlight, temperature extremes), and in compliance with state and federal law.

A program must be in place to review expiration dates regularly, and move any expired, deteriorated, or damaged products to a quarantined area.

Non-prescription drug permittees must notify the Board within ten (10) days of a change in any of the following:
- ✓ Phone number.
- ✓ Facsimile (fax) number.
- ✓ Mailing address.
- ✓ E-mail address.
- ✓ Name of business.

When there is a change in ownership, the prospective owner must submit a completed permit application and fee within 14 days of a change in ownership (involving stock ownership of 30% or more).

To relocate, the permittee must submit an "Application for Relocation" at least 30 days before relocating.

Non-prescription drug permittees must keep records of receipt and disposal for three (3) years. ᴿ⁴⁻²³⁻⁶⁰¹

Non-prescription drug permittees must also comply with state and federal laws pertaining to the retail sale of methamphetamine precursors (e.g. pseudoephedrine sale limits and recordkeeping requirements).

*NON-PRESCRIPTION DRUG VENDING MACHINES

- ✓ Each machine must have a separate Board-issued non-prescription drug permit.
- ✓ A Board-issued identification seal must be affixed to each machine.
- ✓ The identification seal must be visible to the public and contain the following information:
    - ⇨ Board-issued permit number.
    - ⇨ Vending machine serial number.
    - ⇨ Owner's name and phone number.
- ✓ Each machine must be stored inside of a water-tight structure (i.e. building), protected from direct sunlight, and maintained at temperatures within the range of $59 - 86°F$
- ✓ The contents of the machine must be in the manufacturer's original packaging.
- ✓ Board compliance officers (or other authorized officers) may inspect the machine.
    - ⇨ Access to the contents must be provided within 24 hours of a request by the Board.
- ✓ Prior to relocating or discontinuing use of a machine, the owner or manager must notify the Board.

RESIDENT DRUG MANUFACTURER PERMITS
R4-23-604

A current Board-issued drug manufacturer permit is required to manufacture, package, re-package, label, or re-label drug products.

Before a drug manufacturer permit can be issued, the Board must:
1. Approve the permit application.
2. Interview the applicant and manager.
3. Receive a satisfactory facility inspection report from a Board compliance officer.

Drug manufacturer permittees must notify the Executive Director of the Board within 24 hours of a change in:
- Drug list (i.e. drugs manufactured, packaged/re-packaged, or labeled/ re-labeled by the business).
- Ownership. *
- Address.
- Phone number.
- Name of business.
- Manager.

> * For changes in ownership involving stock ownership of 30% or more, the prospective owner must submit a new application prior to the change in ownership.

Drug manufacturer permittees that relocate must submit a new application to the Board prior to relocating; however, there is no application fee when relocating. Issuance of a permit for the new location is contingent upon passing a final inspection conducted by a Board compliance officer.

A change in any officers of a corporation also necessitates the submission of a new application; however, an application fee and final inspection are not necessary when submitting a new application for this purpose.

DRUG DISTRIBUTION RESTRICTIONS

Drug manufacturers must only distribute drugs to properly licensed or permitted individuals and businesses (e.g. medical practitioners, pharmacies, non-prescription drug retailers).

Drug manufacturers are required to comply with current good manufacturing practices (cGMP).

Drug manufacturer permittees must make their manufacturing facilities available for Board inspection.

RESIDENT DRUG WHOLESALER PERMITS
R4-23-605

There are two (2) types of wholesaler permits:
- ✓ Full-service drug wholesale permits.
- ✓ Non-prescription drug wholesale permits.

Before a full-service drug wholesale permit can be issued, the Board must:
1. Approve the permit application.
2. Interview the applicant and designated representative.
3. Receive a satisfactory facility inspection report from a Board compliance officer.

All drug wholesaler permittees must notify the Executive Director of the Board within 24 hours of a change in:
- ✓ Type of drugs sold/distributed.
- ✓ Ownership. *
- ✓ Address.
- ✓ Phone number.
- ✓ Name of business.
- ✓ Manager or designated representative.

> * For changes in ownership involving stock ownership of 30% or more, the prospective owner must submit a new application prior to the change in ownership.

Full-service or non-prescription drug wholesaler permittees that relocate must submit a new application to the Board prior to relocating; however, there is no application fee when relocating. Issuance of a permit for the new location is contingent upon passing a final inspection conducted by a Board compliance officer.

A change in any officers of a corporation also necessitates submission of a new application; however, an application fee and final inspection are not necessary when submitting a new application for this purpose.

DRUG DISTRIBUTION RESTRICTIONS

Drug wholesalers must only distribute drugs to properly licensed or permitted individuals and businesses (e.g. medical practitioners, pharmacies, non-prescription drug retailers).

Drug wholesalers can complete a cash-and-carry sale* only after verifying that:
- ✓ The order is valid.
- ✓ The person picking up the order represents the person or entity that placed the order.
- ✓ The sale is to meet the immediate needs of the person or entity who placed the order (for Rx-only drug orders).

> * Typically, drug orders are delivered to the buyer's location and the cost is credited to their account. In a cash-and-carry sale, the buyer pays for the order up front and makes their own transportation arrangements.

PRODUCTS MUST REMAIN IN MANUFACTURER'S PACKAGING

Full-service and non-prescription drug wholesaler permittees cannot re-package or re-label products. All products must remain as originally packaged and labeled by the manufacturer or re-packager.

FACILITY REQUIREMENTS

Drug wholesale facilities must be:
- ✓ Of adequate size and construction.
- ✓ Well-lighted inside and out.
- ✓ Adequately ventilated.
- ✓ Clean, uncluttered, and sanitary.
- ✓ Equipped with a functional security system to protect against theft.

Access to product storage areas must be restricted to authorized personnel only.

All drugs stocked, sold, or offered for sale must be kept clean, protected from deteriorating factors (e.g. sunlight and temperature extremes), and in compliance with state and federal law and official compendium (i.e. USP and National Formulary) storage requirements.

Temperature and humidity recording devices or logs must be kept in areas where products are stored.

Drug wholesale facilities must be open for Board inspection during regular business hours.

QUARANTINE AREA

Each facility must have a designated quarantine area for storing products that are (or are suspected to be):
- ⇨ Expired, damaged, deteriorated, adulterated, misbranded, counterfeited, or contraband.

Product expiration dates must be reviewed regularly, and any product with less than 120 days remaining until the expiration date must be moved to the quarantine area. Quarantined products must either be destroyed or returned to the source from which they were obtained.

FULL SERVICE WHOLESALE PERMITTEES
ARS § 32-1982 & R4-23-605

Wholesale distributors that distribute drugs within, into, or from Arizona must obtain a permit from the Board.

DESIGNATED REPRESENTATIVE REQUIREMENTS
- ✓ The wholesale permit must identify a "designated representative."
- ✓ To qualify as a potential designated representative, a person must meet all of the following requirements:
  - Be at least 21 years-old.
  - Possess a background including at least three (3) years of employment in a pharmacy or working with a full service wholesale permittee doing tasks such as dispensing, distributing, and recordkeeping with prescription drugs.
  - Be employed by the permittee in a management-level position.
  - Be actively involved in the daily wholesale distribution of prescription drugs.
  - Be physically present at the place of business during regular business hours.
  - Not be serving as the designated representative under another full service wholesale permit.
  - Possess a background clear of any crimes related to Rx-only or controlled substance drug distribution.

FINGERPRINT REQUIREMENT

The Board requires fingerprints from the permit applicant's designated representative for the purpose of performing a state and federal criminal records check.

PHARMACY LAW
SIMPLIFIED

FULL SERVICE WHOLESALER TRANSACTIONS

ARS § 32-1983 & R4-23-605

- ✓ Full service wholesale distributors may furnish prescription drugs to pharmacies and medical practitioners. Prior to completing the transaction, the wholesaler must verify that the pharmacy or practitioner holds a valid license or permit.

- ✓ Full service wholesale distributors must deliver prescription drugs to the location listed on the purchaser's license or permit.

- ✓ When a pharmacy receives prescription drugs from a full service wholesale distributor, any discrepancies between the receipt and the product actually received must be reported to the wholesaler by the next business day.

RETURNS AND EXCHANGES

Full service wholesale distributors can accept Rx-only medication returns or exchanges from a pharmacy or chain pharmacy warehouse, EXCEPT when...
- ✓ The product has been adulterated or counterfeited. *
- ✓ The amount being returned or exchanged exceeds the amount that was sold to the pharmacy.

Unless returned in response to an FDA or manufacturer recall.

When a pharmacy or pharmacy chain warehouse returns or exchanges Rx-only medications to a full service wholesale distributor, documentation of the following must be included:
- ✓ Name, strength, and manufacturer of each product.
- ✓ Statement that the products were stored in compliance with package labeling.

PRESCRIPTION DRUG PEDIGREES
ARS § 32-1984 & R4-23-605

DEFINITION OF PEDIGREE
A pedigree is a document or electronic file that records each instance in which a product is distributed from the time it is obtained from the manufacturer until the time it is sold to a pharmacy or medical practitioner.

INFORMATION CONTAINED IN A PEDIGREE
PRODUCT INFORMATION:
- ✓ Drug name.
- ✓ Dosage form and strength.
- ✓ Container size.
- ✓ Number of containers.
- ✓ Lot number.
- ✓ Manufacturer's name.

TRANSACTION INFORMATION:
- ✓ Name, address, phone number, and e-mail address (if available) of each owner of the Rx-only drug and each wholesaler that handles the drug.
- ✓ Name and address of each location from which the drug was shipped (if different from owner's).
- ✓ Transaction dates.
- ✓ Certification that each recipient has authenticated the pedigree.

RECORDKEEPING REQUIREMENTS FOR FULL SERVICE WHOLESALE DISTRIBUTORS
Full service wholesale distributors must maintain inventory and transaction records, including pedigrees, for all Rx-only medications that leave the normal distribution channel.

Before further distributing an Rx-only medication, the distributor must verify that each transaction listed on the pedigree has actually occurred.

Full service wholesale distributors must maintain the pedigree* and a copy of the license or permit of each person/entity with which they do business. These records must be made available immediately or within two (2) business days upon request from the Board.

*Non-prescription drug wholesalers are not required to maintain pedigrees.

MAINTAIN RECORDS FOR THREE (3) YEARS

Records must be maintained by the full service wholesale distributor and purchaser for at least three (3) years.

NON-RESIDENT PERMITS
R4-23-607

Manufacturers, wholesale distributors, and pharmacies that are not located in Arizona, yet wish to conduct business in Arizona (i.e. sell, distribute, and/or dispense drugs) must obtain a non-resident permit.

TYPES OF NON-RESIDENT PERMITS

- Non-resident pharmacy permit
- Non-resident manufacturer permit
- Non-resident full-service drug wholesale permit
- Non-resident non-prescription drug wholesale permit
- Non-resident non-prescription drug permit

To qualify for a non-resident permit, an entity must possess an equivalent license or permit in the state/jurisdiction where they reside.

BOARD NOTIFICATION REQUIREMENTS

Generally, for non-resident permittees, changes (e.g. address, phone number, name of business, manager) should be communicated to the Board within ten (10) days. The exception is a change in ownership involving stock ownership of 30% or more, in which case the prospective owner must submit a new application before the change occurs.

As of 2015, non-resident pharmacies are no longer required to employ a pharmacist-in-charge who possesses an Arizona pharmacist license.

Non-resident permittees (e.g. manufacturers, wholesalers, retailers, and pharmacies) must only sell/distribute drugs to properly licensed individuals and businesses (e.g. medical practitioners, pharmacies, non-prescription drug retailers). Non-resident pharmacies must only dispense drugs to patients with a valid prescription.

When non-resident permittees sell/distribute drugs, they must keep a copy of the current permit or license of the individual/entity acquiring the drug. This does not apply for pharmacies dispensing drugs pursuant to a valid prescription.

PRODUCTS MUST REMAIN IN MANUFACTURER'S PACKAGING

Non-resident wholesalers (both full-service and non-prescription drug wholesalers) cannot re-package or re-label products. All products must remain as originally packaged and labeled by the manufacturer or re-packager.

When selling/distributing products into Arizona, non-resident permittees must comply with all of the following:
- ✓ Resident state law.
- ✓ Arizona law.
- ✓ Federal law.

UNETHICAL AND UNPROFESSIONAL CONDUCT
ARS § 32-3208 & ARS § 32-3208

EXAMPLES OF UNETHICAL AND UNPROFESSIONAL CONDUCT
- Committing any felony. *
- Committing a misdemeanor that demonstrates moral turpitude. *
- Committing a drug-related misdemeanor. *
- Demonstrating a lack of moral character while exercising privileges granted by a permit.
- Demonstrating an unfitness (e.g. addiction to drugs) that could jeopardize public safety.
- Working while under the influence of drugs or alcohol.
- Violating federal or state pharmacy law or administrative rules.
- Violating federal or state recordkeeping/reporting requirements for precursor substances such as pseudoephedrine.
- Failing to report in writing that...
    - A pharmacist or pharmacy intern is or may be...
        - ✓ Professionally incompetent.
        - ✓ Guilty of unprofessional conduct.
        - ✓ Mentally or physically incapable of practicing pharmacy safely.
    - A pharmacy technician or technician trainee is or may be...
        - ✓ Professionally incompetent.
        - ✓ Guilty of unprofessional conduct.
        - ✓ Mentally or physically incapable of performing duties.
    - A permittee or permittee's employee is or may be...
        - ✓ Guilty of unethical conduct.
        - ✓ Mentally or physically incapable of performing duties safely.
- Selling or distributing counterfeit drugs.
- Obtaining or attempting to obtain a permit by fraudulent means.
- Creating false records or reports.
- Providing false or misleading information to the Board.
- Omitting information when communicating with the Board.
- Interfering with agents attempting to conduct an inspection (e.g. preventing access to the pharmacy or failing to provide access to records).
- Failing to respond/comply with a subpoena from the Board.
- Failing to notify the Board when there is a change in ownership, management, or pharmacist-in-charge.
- Claiming to have performed a service that was not actually performed.
- Charging a fee for a service that was not actually provided.
- Using false or misleading methods or information to advertise drugs, devices, or services.
- Dispensing a brand of medication other than what was prescribed without obtaining permission from the prescribing practitioner (except when performing generic substitution).
- Knowingly dispensing a prescription drug without a valid prescription.
- Claiming professional superiority in relation to compounding or dispensing.
- Noncompliance with continuing education (CE) requirements.
- Filling prescriptions issued after a diagnosis is made by way of the mail or internet. **
- Paying rebates (or agreeing to pay rebates) to a health care provider.
- Providing practitioners with Rx pads/blanks that display or identify the pharmacist's or pharmacy's name, address, etc.
- Failing to report a change in residency status, home address, or employer to the Board.

* Based on a conviction or plea of nolo contendere (no contest).
** The pharmacist may fill fill such a prescription in cases where the prescriber is issuing a prescription to...
- Provide temporary medical supervision on behalf of the regular provider.
- Fulfill a consultation requested by the regular provider.
- Respond to an emergency medical situation.
- Prepare the patient for a medical exam (e.g. PEG-3350 for a colonoscopy).
- A person who was possibly exposed to a communicable disease (e.g. HIV/AIDS).
- A patient of a legitimate telemedicine program.
- A household member of a patient for a CDC-recommended immunization.
- A school district or charter school for a stock of emergency-use epinephrine auto-injectors.
- Be used by a county or tribal public health department for...
  - ✓ Immunization programs.
  - ✓ Emergency treatment.
  - ✓ Response to an infectious disease outbreak or investigation.
  - ✓ Response to an act of bioterrorism.

Note: A "licensee" is a person with a license; for instance, a licensed pharmacist or pharmacy technician. On the other hand, a "permittee" is a person with a permit; for instance, a person with a permit to operate a pharmacy.

COMMITTING A FELONY OR MISDEMEANOR – BOARD NOTIFICATION REQUIREMENT

Licensed or certified health professionals* must notify their licensing/certifying Board in writing within 10 days after being charged with any felony or a misdemeanor that potentially affects patient safety.

* Includes individuals who have applied for a license or certificate that have not yet been licensed or certified.

✓ The Board may follow up with an investigation.

✓ Noncompliance with this notification requirement is considered to be an act of "unprofessional conduct" that is punishable by a fine of up to $1,000 +/- other disciplinary actions (e.g. deny application for licensure).

UNETHICAL PRACTICES
R4-23-404

✓ Compensating medical practitioners or facilities in exchange for referrals or prescriptions.
✓ Advertising on prescription blanks.
✓ Claiming the performance of services that were not actually performed.
✓ Selling Rx-only drugs or devices without a valid prescription.
✓ Dispensing Rx-only drugs or devices pursuant to a diagnosis made via the mail or internet. *

* Exceptions are noted after the double asterisk (**) at the top of this page.

PROHIBITED ACTS
ARS § 32-1965

✓ Manufacturing, selling, holding, or offering for sale any product that is adulterated or misbranded.
✓ Adulterating or misbranding a product.
✓ Destroying any part of a label on a drug, device, poison, or hazardous substance that is offered for sale.
✓ Manufacturing, selling, holding, or offering for sale any counterfeit drug.
✓ Creating or offering to create forged prescriptions.
✓ Practicing pharmacy without a license.

ADULTERATED DRUGS AND DEVICES
ARS § 32-1966

Definition of an "adulterated" drug product or device:
- ✓ Consists of any filthy, putrid, or decomposed substance.
- ✓ Produced, prepared, packed, or stored under unsanitary conditions.
- ✓ Not produced, prepared, packed, or stored in accordance with good manufacturing practices.
- ✓ The container is made of a substance that could render the contents injurious to health.
- ✓ The product contains a coloring agent that has been deemed unsafe.
- ✓ The strength differs from, or the quality or purity falls below, that which is stated on the label.

MISBRANDED DRUGS AND DEVICES
ARS § 32-1967

Definition of a "misbranded" drug product or device:
- ✓ Labeling is false or misleading.
- ✓ The label does not identify the name and location of either the manufacturer, packer, or distributor.
- ✓ The label does not accurately state the quantity of contents in terms of weight, measure, or numerical count.
- ✓ A legally-required word or statement is not displayed on the label or in the labeling.
- ✓ A product for human use that contains a certain habit-forming substance (e.g. narcotic or hypnotic substance) without indicating the name and quantity of said substance on the label.
- ✓ Drugs with a label that does not identify the established name and quantity of the active ingredient(s). *
- ✓ Labeling does not include adequate directions for use and adequate warnings.
- ✓ The product is an imitation of another drug or device.
- ✓ The product is offered for sale under the name of another drug or device.
- ✓ The product is dangerous to health if used used as prescribed, recommended, or suggested in the labeling.
- ✓ Per ARS § 32-1968, a prescription-only drug that fails to bear the statement "Rx only" at any time prior to dispensing.

*Including the concentration of alcohol (if present in the formulation).

BOARD DISCIPLINE FOR PHARMACISTS, PHARMACY INTERNS, AND GRADUATE INTERNS
ARS § 32-1927 & ARS § 32-1928

Pharmacists, pharmacy interns, and graduate interns may be disciplined by the Board for:
- ✓ Unprofessional conduct.
- ✓ Results of a psychiatric exam that deem the licensee unfit to practice pharmacy.
- ✓ Physical or mental inability to practice pharmacy safely.
- ✓ Professional incompetence.
- ✓ Using a license issued in error.

Anyone MAY report potential cases of unprofessional conduct, professional incompetence, or physical or mental inability to practice pharmacy safely, but for licensees and permittees it is not optional. If a licensee or permittee is aware of such cases, they MUST report them to the Board. Failing to report such cases is in itself an act of unprofessional conduct that is subject to disciplinary action. Anyone who reports information IN GOOD FAITH is NOT subject to civil liability.

At the licensee's expense, the Board may require a licensee to undergo assessment by a Board-approved substance abuse and rehabilitation program.

If a licensee is terminated for unprofessional conduct, professional incompetence, or for being mentally or physically unable to practice pharmacy safely, then the permittee or pharmacist-in-charge must inform the Board and provide a statement of the reason(s) for termination. The Board must also be informed if a licensee resigns while under investigation.

DISCIPLINARY ACTIONS
After formal hearing(s), any licensee found guilty of unprofessional conduct, professional incompetence, or of being mentally or physically incapable of practicing pharmacy safely may be disciplined by way of...
- ✓ A civil penalty (including fines of up to $1,000 per violation).
- ✓ A letter of reprimand.
- ✓ A decree of censure (an official action that may require restitution of fees to the affected patient(s)).
- ✓ A requirement to complete Board-designated CE courses.
- ✓ Probation.
- ✓ Suspension or revocation of a license.

Note: In addition to the prescribed discipline, the Board may also require the licensee to pay the costs associated with formal hearing(s).

EMERGENCY LICENSE RESTRICTION OR SUSPENSION
If a licensee poses a threat to public health, welfare, and safety, then the Board may take emergency action to restrict or suspend a license immediately until proceedings for revocation or other action can take place.

BOARD DISCIPLINE FOR PHARMACY TECHNICIANS AND PHARMACY TECHNICIAN TRAINEES
ARS § 32-1927.01

Pharmacy technicians and pharmacy technician trainees may be disciplined by the Board for...
- ✓ Unprofessional conduct.
- ✓ Results of a psychiatric exam that deem the licensee unfit to perform employment duties.
- ✓ Physical or mental inability to perform employment duties safely.
- ✓ Professional incompetence.
- ✓ Using a license issued in error.

Pharmacy technicians are subjected to the same general types of discipline as pharmacists, pharmacy interns, and graduate interns as outlined on the previous page.

BOARD DISCIPLINE FOR PHARMACY PERMITTEES
ARS § 32-1927.02

A permittee may be disciplined by the Board if...
- ✓ The permittee or an employee of the permittee commits an act of unethical conduct.
- ✓ The permittee or an employee of the permittee is deemed unfit by a psychiatric examination.
- ✓ The permittee or an employee of the permittee is physically or mentally unable to perform employment duties safely.
- ✓ The permit was issued in error.
- ✓ The permittee or an employee of the permittee allows a person without the necessary license (i.e. pharmacist, graduate intern, pharmacy intern, pharmacy technician, pharmacy technician trainee) to work in the pharmacy.

Permittees are subject to the same general types of discipline as licensees (pharmacists, technicians, etc.). For instance, the Board may restrict, suspend, or revoke a permit as a method of discipline.

BOARD HEARINGS
R4-23-111, R4-23-113, R4-23-119, R4-23-122, R4-23-126, R4-23-128

License or permit revocations, suspensions, probation, or fines will be implemented only after notice* is served and a hearing is conducted, UNLESS a licensee or permittee is guilty of deliberate and willful violations, or violations that pose an immediate threat to the public health, safety, or welfare.

> * The Board must give notice to the licensee or permittee at least 30 days before the set date for the hearing.

- ✓ All hearings are open to the public.
- ✓ The Board has the authority to order disruptive individuals to leave or be removed from the hearing.

MOTION FOR RULING
The following rulings may be requested by submitting a written motion to the Board at least 15 days before the set date of the hearing:
- ☐ Continuing or expediting a hearing.
- ☐ Vacating a hearing (i.e. canceling a hearing).
- ☐ Scheduling a pre-hearing conference (e.g. to outline the issues to be discussed at the hearing).
- ☐ Quashing a subpoena. *
- ☐ Requesting telephonic testimony (e.g. if attending the hearing poses undue hardship for a party or witness).
- ☐ Reconsidering a previous order.

> * The Board must quash a subpoena if it is unreasonable or oppressive, or if the testimony or evidence sought may be obtained by some other method.

REHEARING OR REVIEW AND APPEAL OF DECISION
The Board may grant a rehearing or review for reasons such as...
- ✓ New evidence.
- ✓ Excessive penalty.
- ✓ Insufficient penalty.
- ✓ Prejudice of Board members.

SUBSTANCE ABUSE TREATMENT AND REHABILITATION PROGRAM

ARS § 32-1932.01 & R4-23-415

- ✓ Established by the Board to treat and rehabilitate licensees impaired by alcohol or drug abuse.
- ✓ Funded by using up to $20 from each biennial license renewal fee collected by the Board.
- ✓ Participants in the treatment and rehabilitation program are either "known" or "confidential."
- ✓ If self-referred, the patient will be "confidential" and remain unidentified to the Board.
- ✓ If ordered by the Board to participate in the program, the patient is "known."

REQUIRED COMPONENTS OF THE PROGRAM
- ✓ Education.
- ✓ Intervention.
- ✓ Therapeutic treatment.
- ✓ Post-treatment monitoring and support.

CONTRACTOR REQUIREMENTS
Implementation of this program may be contracted out to other organizations. If contracted out to a private organization, the contract must include each of the following:
- ☐ Periodic activity reports to the Board.
- ☐ Release of all treatment records to the Board pursuant to a written request.
- ☐ Quarterly reports to the Board including each participant's diagnosis, prognosis, and recommendations.
- ☐ A requirement to immediately report to the Board the identity of any participant believed to pose a danger to self or others.
- ☐ A requirement to report to the Board as soon as possible the identity of any person who refuses treatment, violates the terms of their contract, or does not improve with treatment.

RECORD REQUESTS
The Board may submit a written request for the treatment records of any participant, and the program administrator must supply the requested records within ten (10) working days.

PRESCRIPTION REQUIREMENTS
R4-23-407

This information must appear on a prescription order for the prescription to be dispensed by a pharmacist...
- ✓ Date written.
- ✓ Name and address of patient (if patient is an animal, then use the name and address of the owner).
- ✓ Drug name, strength, and dosage form.
    - ⇨ For devices, only the name of the device is necessary.
- ✓ Manufacturer's or distributor's name if written for generic or if generic substitution is performed.
- ✓ Directions for use.
- ✓ Date of dispensing.
- ✓ Quantity prescribed and quantity dispensed.
- ✓ DEA number of prescriber (only required for controlled substance prescriptions).
- ✓ Prescriber's authorization to dispense as indicated by the:
    - ⇨ Prescriber's signature if the prescription is written (as opposed to electronic or oral).
    - ⇨ Prescriber's electronic or digital signature if the prescription is electronic.
    - ⇨ Prescriber's name and phone number if the prescription is orally communicated.
- ✓ Name or initials of the dispensing pharmacist.

PRESCRIPTION REFILL DOCUMENTATION REQUIREMENTS
This information must be recorded on the back of a prescription order to document the dispensing of refills:
- ✓ Date refilled.
- ✓ Quantity dispensed.
- ✓ Manufacturer's or distributor's name (or abbreviation) if generic is dispensed.
- ✓ Name or initials of the dispensing pharmacist.

PRESCRIPTION RECORD MAINTENANCE

Pharmacies must keep prescription orders on file for at least seven (7) years from the most recent date of dispensing.

A pharmacist may provide a copy of a prescription order to a patient or his/her authorized agent as long as the copy displays a statement to the effect of "COPY FOR REFERENCE PURPOSES ONLY."

PRESCRIPTION TRANSFER DOCUMENTATION REQUIREMENTS
TRANSFERRING PHARMACY (THE PHARMACY THAT LAST FILLED THE PRESCRIPTION)
The pharmacist or intern must invalidate the original prescription order by writing "VOID" on the face of the original prescription, or the prescription information must be invalidated in the computer. Additionally, the following information must be recorded on the back of the original prescription order or in the pharmacy's computer system:
- ✓ Receiving pharmacy's name and ID code, number, or address.
- ✓ Receiving pharmacy's telephone number.
- ✓ Name of pharmacist or intern receiving the transfer.
- ✓ Name of the pharmacist or intern transferring the prescription out.

RECEIVING PHARMACY (THE PHARMACY THAT WILL FILL THE PRESCRIPTION NEXT)
The pharmacist or intern receiving the prescription transfer must record:
- ✓ The word "TRANSFER."
- ✓ Date of issuance for the original prescription order.
- ✓ Original number of refills authorized.
- ✓ Date initially dispensed.
- ✓ Number of refills remaining and date of last refill.
- ✓ Transferring pharmacy's name and ID code, number, or address.
- ✓ Transferring pharmacy's telephone number.
- ✓ Rx number for the original prescription order.
- ✓ Name of the pharmacist or intern transferring the prescription out.
- ✓ Name of pharmacist or intern receiving the transfer.

Note: For controlled substance prescriptions, each pharmacy must record the other pharmacy's DEA number.

OTHER IMPORTANT POINTS REGARDING PRESCRIPTION TRANSFERS

- ✓ Only licensed pharmacists, pharmacy interns, and graduate interns can communicate a transfer by phone.

- ✓ Schedule III and IV controlled substance prescriptions can only be transferred between two (2) licensed pharmacists (i.e. cannot be transferred by interns).

- ✓ Electronic transfers are permitted between pharmacies under common ownership that use a common or shared database.

- ✓ Non-controlled substance prescriptions can be transferred ELECTRONICALLY by pharmacists, pharmacy interns, graduate interns, pharmacy technicians, and pharmacy technician trainees. *

    *As always, when non-pharmacist personnel perform a task,
    the task must be completed under pharmacist supervision.

- ✓ Non-controlled substance prescriptions can be transferred without limitation up to the number of refills authorized on the original prescription.

- ✓ Controlled substance prescriptions can be transferred electronically ONLY between two (2) licensed pharmacists.

- ✓ Controlled substance prescriptions can be transferred on a one-time basis; however, if both pharmacies share a real-time online database, then prescriptions can be transferred without limitation up to the number of refills authorized on the original prescription.

- ✓ The original and the transferred prescription orders must be kept on file at the respective pharmacies for seven (7) years from the date of last dispensing.

PHARMACY LAW SIMPLIFIED

PRESCRIPTIONS FAXED FROM A PRACTITIONER TO A PHARMACY

A practitioner or his/her agent may fax prescription orders to the patient's pharmacy of choice for:
- ✓ Schedule III, IV, and V controlled substances.
- ✓ Rx-only drugs.
- ✓ Non-prescription drugs.

Note: Schedule II controlled substance prescriptions may be faxed for informational purposes only. *

> * Exceptions include prescriptions for home infusion, long-term care, and hospice patients. In these cases, the faxed prescription may serve as the original prescription for recordkeeping purposes. ARS § 36-2525

Prescriptions must be faxed from:
- ✓ A practitioner's practice location.
- ✓ A nurse at a hospital, long-term care facility, or inpatient hospice facility if for a patient of the facility.

In addition to the normal information required to appear on a prescription (per ARS § 32-1968; see page 41), for a faxed prescription to be valid, the following additional information must be included:
- ✓ Date faxed.
- ✓ Fax number and phone number of the location from which the fax was sent.
- ✓ Name of the person who sent the fax (if sent by someone other than the practitioner).

Refill authorizations may be faxed from a practitioner or his/her agent to the pharmacy as long as the following information is included:
- ✓ Date of authorization.
- ✓ Practitioner's signature OR the name of the practitioner's agent who sent the fax.
- ✓ Practitioner's phone number and fax number.

E-PRESCRIBING CONTROLLED SUBSTANCES

Prescriptions for Schedule II, III, IV, and V controlled substances may be issued electronically (i.e. "e-prescribed") as long as the systems comply with federal law.

As with faxed prescriptions, electronic prescriptions should only be transmitted to the patient's pharmacy of choice.

In addition to the normal information required to appear on a prescription (per ARS § 32-1968; see page 41), for an e-prescription to be valid, the following additional information must be included:
- ✓ Date transmitted.
- ✓ Name of the person who transmitted the prescription (if sent by someone other than the practitioner).

DISPENSING PRESCRIPTION DRUGS
ARS § 32-1968

Pharmacies may accept prescriptions in any of the following formats:
- ✓ Written on paper with the prescriber's manual signature.
- ✓ Electronic with the prescriber's electronic or digital signature.
  - ⇨ Must be promptly reduced to writing and filed by the pharmacist.
- ✓ Generated electronically on paper with the prescriber's electronic or manual signature.
  - ⇨ If signed electronically, must be printed on security paper to preclude copying or alteration.
- ✓ Oral (i.e. via telephone) as long as it is promptly reduced to writing and filed by the pharmacist.
- ✓ Faxed or e-mailed directly from the prescriber or the prescriber's agent (e.g. a nurse or secretary).

PRESCRIPTIONS SENT BY THE PATIENT VIA FAX OR E-MAIL

Prescriptions faxed or e-mailed by the patient may be filled, but may not be dispensed until the patient presents the original written prescription that contains the prescriber's manual signature.

Information required to appear on a PRESCRIPTION ORDER:
- ✓ Date written/issued.
- ✓ Name and address of the patient (for animals, the owner's name and address should be used).
- ✓ Number of refills authorized (if any).
- ✓ Name, address, and phone number of the prescriber.
- ✓ Name, strength, dosage form, and quantity of the prescribed medication.
- ✓ Directions for use.

PRESCRIPTION EXPIRATION

Prescriptions cannot be refilled more than one (1) year after the date written.

Information required to appear on the LABEL of a prescription that is dispensed to a patient:
- ✓ Pharmacy's name and address.
- ✓ Serial number ("Rx number").
- ✓ Date of dispensing.
- ✓ Prescriber's name.
- ✓ Patient's name (for animals, the owner's name and the species of the animal).
- ✓ Directions for use.
- ✓ Any cautionary statements contained in the order.

FOREIGN PRESCRIPTIONS
ARS § 32-1969

A new prescription order issued by a practitioner licensed by the licensing board of a foreign country may be filled UNLESS the prescription is for a controlled substance.

GENERIC SUBSTITUTION
ARS § 32-1963.01

Unless the prescriber indicates he/she intends to prevent substitution, a pharmacist may dispense a generic equivalent when the prescriber issues a brand name prescription.

A pharmacist must dispense the brand name if the order contains a statement that clearly intends to prevent generic substitution, such as "DAW," "dispense as written," "do not substitute," or "brand medically necessary."

PATIENT NOTIFICATION REQUIREMENTS
When dispensing a generic equivalent for a patient without third party reimbursement, pharmacy personnel must notify the person presenting the prescription of the price difference between the prescribed brand name drug and the generic equivalent.

When dispensing a generic substitute, the prescription label must state "generic equivalent for [INSERT BRAND NAME]."

> **Note:** These requirements do not apply to pharmacies serving patients in health care institutions (including hospitals with a formulary).

PROFESSIONAL JUDGEMENT
An employer cannot require a pharmacist to select a specific generic equivalent. Selection of an appropriate generic equivalent depends on the order of the prescriber or the professional judgement of the pharmacist.

EXPIRATION DATE REQUIREMENT
Generic equivalents WITHOUT AN EXPIRATION DATE printed on the stock bottle label CANNOT be dispensed.

NO INCREASED LEGAL LIABILITY
Performing generic substitution does not expose a pharmacist to increased legal liability.

B-RATED DRUG PRODUCTS CANNOT BE DISPENSED AS GENERIC EQUIVALENTS
According to Arizona statutes, a drug with unresolved bioequivalence concerns (i.e. drugs with B-rated therapeutic equivalence codes according to the Orange Book) CANNOT be considered "generically equivalent" to the brand name drug.

PRESCRIPTION RECORDS
ARS § 32-1964

- ✓ The proprietor, manager, or pharmacist-in-charge must maintain a book or file in the pharmacy that contains every prescription order for drugs, devices, or replacement soft contact lenses compounded or dispensed by the pharmacy.

- ✓ Each order must be serially numbered, dated, and filed in the order they were compounded or dispensed.

- ✓ Rather than using a hardcopy filing system, these records may be stored in a retrievable format using an electronic imaging recordkeeping system. For painstaking details regarding the electronic imaging system requirements, see Arizona Administrative Code Title 4, Chapter 23-408 (H).

STORAGE OF PRESCRIPTION ORDER RECORDS

Each prescription order must be maintained for at least seven (7) years. Prescribers, the Board, agents of the Board, and officers of the law may inspect these records at any time as necessary to perform their duties.

RETURNING DRUGS AND DEVICES
R4-23-409

Once a drug has been sold/dispensed and leaves the pharmacy, it CANNOT be returned or exchanged for resale UNLESS the drug is unopened in the manufacturer's original container AND otherwise protected from contamination and deterioration.

Note: This does not apply to hospitals or long-term care facilities.

Once a device has been sold/dispensed and left the premises, it CANNOT be returned or exchanged for resale UNLESS all of the following conditions are true of the device in question:
- ✓ Free of defects.
- ✓ Incapable of transferring disease.
- ✓ If resold or reused, not claimed to be new or unused.

PHARMACY QUALITY ASSURANCE PROGRAMS
ARS § 32-1973 & R4-23-620

- ✓ Every pharmacy must have a continuous quality assurance (CQA) program to address medication errors.
- ✓ Compliance with the CQA program must be documented.
- ✓ Documentation must be maintained for at least two (2) years.
- ✓ Medication error data generated by the CQA program must be reviewed on a regular basis.
- ✓ Records are "peer review documents" and cannot be used in legal disputes or civil proceedings.
- ✓ Compliance with the CQA program is a mitigating factor in the Board investigation of a medication error.

CQA POLICIES AND PROCEDURES

The pharmacy permittee or pharmacist-in-charge is responsible for ensuring that a pharmacy prepares, implements, and complies with policies and procedures for a continuous quality assurance (CQA) program. These policies and procedures must address:
- ✓ Training of pharmacy personnel.
- ✓ Detection and documentation of medication errors.
- ✓ Use of data to assess causes and contributing factors for medication errors.
- ✓ Improvement of patient care quality.
- ✓ Use of findings to develop/change systems and workflow to prevent/reduce errors.
- ✓ Communication with pharmacy personnel annually (at minimum) to review findings and changes.

As with all other pharmacy policies and procedures, the policies and procedures related to a pharmacy's continuous quality assurance (CQA) program must be...
- ✓ Assembled into a manual (written or electronic).
- ✓ Made available for employee reference and Board inspection.
- ✓ Reviewed and, if necessary, changed/updated biennially (once every two (2) years).

PATIENT COUNSELING REQUIREMENTS
R4-23-402

Only pharmacists or interns can counsel patients or caregivers about a prescription medication on an outpatient basis (including patients discharged from a hospital).

SITUATIONS THAT REQUIRE ORAL CONSULTATION
- ✓ New prescription.
- ✓ New strength, dosage form, or directions.
- ✓ Pharmacist determines that consultation is warranted (this would be based on professional judgement).
- ✓ Patient or patient's caregiver requests oral consultation.

REQUIRED ELEMENTS OF ORAL CONSULTATION
- ✓ Name and strength of the medication (or name of device).
- ✓ Labeled indication.
- ✓ Directions for use.
- ✓ Route of administration.
- ✓ Special instructions.

+ Written information regarding side effects, procedures for missed doses, or storage requirements.

PROFESSIONAL JUDGEMENT
The pharmacist or intern may exercise professional judgement in deciding whether or not to include the following additional information during oral consultation:
- ☐ Common severe side effects (and action to take if they occur), interactions, and/or contraindications.
- ☐ Self-monitoring techniques.
- ☐ Duration of therapy.
- ☐ Refill information.

Oral consultation may be omitted if necessary using professional judgement. In these cases, the pharmacist or intern must personally provide written information that would normally be discussed during an oral consultation and provide a method to contact a pharmacist or intern at a later time (e.g. the pharmacy phone number). The pharmacist or intern must also document the circumstance and reason for not consulting orally.

CONSULTATION REFUSED
Oral consultation is not required if a patient or caregiver refuses consultation.

DOCUMENTATION REQUIREMENTS
- ✓ Must document whether or not oral consultation is provided. Documentation must include the name, initials, or other ID code of the responsible pharmacist or intern.
- ✓ Whenever oral consultation is not provided, the circumstance and reason must be documented.

PRESCRIPTION DELIVERY
When a prescription is delivered and the pharmacist is not present, the following medication information must accompany the prescription in written or printed form:
- ✓ Approved uses.
- ✓ Potential side effects.
- ✓ Potential drug interactions.
- ✓ Action to take in the event of a missed dose.
- ✓ Phone number of the dispensing pharmacy to consult with a pharmacist.

PHARMACIST-ADMINISTERED IMMUNIZATIONS
ARS § 32-1974 & R4-23-411

✓ Licensed pharmacists and interns may administer immunizations in Arizona if certified by the Board.

ADMINISTRATION OF IMMUNIZATIONS BY INTERNS

Licensed pharmacy interns and graduate interns certified to administer immunizations can only do so under the direct supervision of a licensed pharmacist certified to administer immunizations.

✓ Pharmacists and interns who are certified to administer immunizations also have the authority to administer emergency medications (epinephrine & diphenhydramine) for immunization-related acute allergic reactions.

✓ Pharmacists and interns who are certified to administer immunizations and emergency epinephrine and diphenhydramine cannot delegate the task of administering these products.

✓ Current immunization certificates must be kept available for Board inspection or public review.

RENEWAL OF PHARMACIST IMMUNIZATION CERTIFICATES

Certificates for pharmacists be renewed every five (5) years. To be eligible for renewal, a pharmacist must:

✓ Maintain current basic CPR certification.
✓ Complete five (5) contact hours (0.5 CEUs) on topics related to immunizations.

ELIGIBILITY REQUIREMENTS FOR A PHARMACIST OR INTERN TO OBTAIN AN IMMUNIZATION CERTIFICATE:
✓ Current licensure as an Arizona pharmacist, pharmacy intern, or graduate intern.
✓ Current certification in basic cardiopulmonary resuscitation (CPR).
✓ Successful completion of an immunization training program. *

➡ *THE IMMUNIZATION TRAINING PROGRAM MUST COVER THE FOLLOWING TOPICS:
✓ Basic immunology & human immune response.
✓ Mechanics of immunity, adverse effects, doses, and vaccine administration schedules.
✓ Emergency administration of epinephrine & diphenhydramine for severe allergic reactions.
✓ Administration of intramuscular injections and other methods of administration.
✓ Recordkeeping and reporting requirements.

PHARMACY LAW
SIMPLIFIED

IMMUNIZATIONS/VACCINES APPROVED FOR ADMINISTRATION BY A PHARMACIST *

≥13 y/o

ADULTS **WITHOUT** A PRESCRIPTION, any immunization or vaccine recommended in either of the following:
- ✓ CDC's recommended adult immunization schedule.
- ✓ CDC's health information for international travel.

ADULTS **WITH** A PRESCRIPTION, any immunization listed in A.A.C. R9-6-1301, which includes the following:
- ✓ Japanese encephalitis vaccine.
- ✓ Rabies vaccine.
- ✓ Typhoid vaccine.
- ✓ Yellow fever vaccine.

3-12

CHILDREN & ADOLESCENTS 6—18 YEARS OF AGE** **WITHOUT** A PRESCRIPTION:
- ✓ An immunization or vaccine for influenza.
- ✓ An immunization or vaccine in response to a public health emergency declared by the Governor.

3-12

CHILDREN & ADOLESCENTS 6—18 YEARS OF AGE** **WITH** A PRESCRIPTION:
- ✓ An immunization or vaccine pursuant to the rules and protocols adopted by the Board.

* Or by an intern under direct supervision of a licensed pharmacist certified to administer immunizations.
** The consent of a parent/guardian is required for any patient under 18 years of age.

RECORDKEEPING REQUIREMENTS
- ✓ Patient's name, address, and date of birth.
- ✓ Date of administration.
- ✓ Site of injection.
- ✓ Name of the immunization, epinephrine, or diphenhydramine.
- ✓ Dose administered.
- ✓ Manufacturer's lot number and expiration date.
- ✓ Name and address of the patient's primary care provider (PCP) or physician.
- ✓ Name of the pharmacist or intern administering the immunization.
- ✓ Documentation of the pharmacist's or (intern's) consultation with the patient by which the patient was deemed eligible for immunization.
- ✓ Professional information provided to the patient by the pharmacist or intern.
- ✓ Name and date of the vaccine information sheet (VIS) given to the patient.
- ✓ Consent form signed by a parent or guardian (for eligible minor patients only).

REPORTING REQUIREMENTS

- ✓ Report the information documented in compliance with the recordkeeping requirements (above) to the patient's PCP or physician (if applicable) within 48 hours after the immunization is administered.

- ✓ Report the administration of adult immunizations to any adult immunization information systems or vaccine registries established by the department of health services.

- ✓ Report adverse events to the federal Vaccine Adverse Event Reporting System (VAERS).

- ✓ Records must be kept by the pharmacy for seven (7) years from the date of immunization.
  - ✓ As with other health information, immunization records must be kept confidential.

IMPLEMENTING, MONITORING, AND MODIFYING DRUG THERAPY
ARS § 32-1970

Pharmacists can implement, monitor, and modify drug therapy if following a written drug therapy management protocol that is prescribed by the provider* who made the diagnosis.

> * A licensed physician or a registered nurse practitioner acting as a primary care provider.

A written drug therapy management protocol must specify all of the following:
- ✓ The drugs to be managed by the pharmacist.
- ✓ Events that require notification of the provider.
- ✓ The lab tests that may be ordered by the pharmacist.

PROVIDER-PATIENT RELATIONSHIP REQUIREMENT
A legitimate provider-patient relationship must exist for a provider to enter into a protocol-based drug therapy agreement.

DISPENSING REPLACEMENT SOFT CONTACT LENSES
ARS § 32-1976

PRESCRIPTION REQUIREMENTS
Prescription orders for replacement soft contact lenses must include:
- ✓ Name of the prescribing physician or optometrist.
- ✓ Date issued.
- ✓ Lens brand name, type, tint, and any other necessary specifications.

SUBSTITUTION PROHIBITED
The pharmacist MUST dispense the exact lenses prescribed – no substitutions.

REFILL LIMITS
Refills dispensed within 60 days of the expiration date of the prescription order are limited to the quantity sufficient to last just through the expiration date. *Do Not go Beyond Expire Date*

PRESCRIPTION EXPIRATION
The expiration date of the prescription order must be the earlier of the expiration date written on the prescription order or one year from the date of issuance.

STATEMENT REQUIRED TO APPEAR ON DISPENSED PRESCRIPTION REPLACEMENT SOFT CONTACT LENSES
"Warning: if you are having any unexplained eye discomfort, watering, vision change or redness, remove your lenses immediately and consult your eye care practitioner before wearing your lenses again."

DECLARED STATE OF EMERGENCY
ARS § 32-1910 & R4-23-412

DURING A STATE OF EMERGENCY, PHARMACISTS MAY PROVIDE ONE-TIME 30-DAY EMERGENCY REFILLS.

PROCEDURE FOR DISPENSING EMERGENCY REFILLS

State of emergency is declared after a natural disaster or terrorist attack.

⇩

Patients are unable to obtain existing prescription refills as a result of the emergency (includes patients that have been temporarily relocated to Arizona during an emergency).

⇩

The pharmacist believes a refill is essential to the maintenance of life or to the continuation of therapy.

⇩

The pharmacist must make a good faith effort to reduce the prescription information to a written prescription marked "emergency prescription" and keep the prescription on file with the other prescription records.

⇩

If the state of emergency continues for 21 days or more after the one-time emergency refill was issued, the pharmacist may issue a second 30-day "one-time" emergency refill.

⇩

When the state of emergency is terminated, the pharmacist must discontinue dispensing emergency refills.

OUT-OF-STATE LICENSEE PARTICIPATION

Pharmacists licensed in a state other than Arizona may participate in a legitimate relief effort during a state of emergency in Arizona, as long as they are able to provide proof of licensure in another state. Out-of-state pharmacy technicians and pharmacy interns working under the supervision of a pharmacist can do this as well.

PHARMACY LAW
SIMPLIFIED

PRESCRIPTION DRUG DONATION PROGRAMS

ARS § 32-1909, R4-23-1202 through 1211

Prescription drugs that are unopened and in their original sealed, tamper-evident packaging (including unit dose medications as long as innermost packaging is intact) may be accepted and dispensed by physician offices, pharmacies, and hospitals.

DRUGS **NOT** ACCEPTABLE FOR DONATION:
- ✓ Controlled substances.
- ✓ Drug samples.
- ✓ Drugs that can only be dispensed to patients registered with the manufacturer.
- ✓ Expired drugs or drugs that will expire within 6 months of donation. *[handwritten: different from 120 days for drug wholesalers]*
- ✓ Adulterated drugs.

⬇

The term ADULTERATED is defined in ARS § 32-1966.
A summary of conditions that would render a drug product "adulterated" is presented below...
- ✓ Consists of any filthy, putrid, or decomposed substance.
- ✓ Produced, prepared, packed, or stored under unsanitary conditions.
- ✓ Not produced, prepared, packed, or stored in accordance with good manufacturing practices.
- ✓ The container is made of a substance that could render the contents injurious to health.
- ✓ The product contains a coloring agent that has been deemed unsafe.
- ✓ The strength differs from, or the quality or purity falls below, that which is stated on the label. *[handwritten: expired/recalled drugs, adulterated drugs]*

The donor of a drug may be an individual*, a manufacturer, or a health care institution.

> * A drug CANNOT be donated by an individual AFTER he/she takes possession of the drug. The drug must be donated through the individual's practitioner, pharmacy or health care institution.

The entity donating a drug must sign a donor form and create an invoice to document the donation. Copies of the invoice and donor form must be sent to the entity receiving the donation. Both parties must maintain these records for at least three (3) years.

Medications that have been accepted as donations can only be dispensed pursuant to a valid prescription to patients who meet eligibility criteria.

Donated medications may be dispensed directly to patients or through a government or non-profit entity.

Prior to dispensing, the pharmacist-in-charge or physician-in-charge of the entity providing the donation must ensure that the donated product has not been adulterated and certify the drug has been stored in compliance with the requirements outlined in the package labeling.

Entities participating in a drug donation program must develop policies and procedures for the receipt, storage, and distribution of donated medications.

Entities/persons participating in a drug donation program are immune from civil liability and professional discipline.

Each patient who receives a donated drug must sign a recipient form to document the receipt of a donation and to document that they understand the immunity provisions of the program.

The patient may be charged a handling fee since there are costs associated with inspection, storage, and dispensing of donated medications. This fee cannot exceed $4.50/prescription.

If needed, donated drugs can be transferred to another participating physician's office, pharmacy, or health care institution. Transfers must be documented on an invoice and copies must be maintained by each party for at least three (3) years.

Donated prescription drugs CANNOT be resold.

Donated drugs that are expired, adulterated, unidentifiable, or recalled must be destroyed within 30 days of identification of the problem. Drugs identified for destruction must be documented on a list. After the drugs are destroyed, the list must be signed by a witness to verify destruction. This list must be kept for at least three (3) years from the date of destruction. R4-23-1211

PATIENT ELIGIBILITY CRITERIA
- ✓ Resident of Arizona.
- ✓ Annual family income ≤ 300% of the poverty level.
- ✓ One of the following:
    - ☐ Does NOT have health insurance.
    - ☐ Has health insurance that does not pay for the drug prescribed.
    - ☐ American or Alaska Native eligible to receive medications through the Indian Health Services, but chooses not to participate.
    - ☐ American or Alaska Native who does NOT have health insurance or has health insurance that does not pay for the drug prescribed.
    - ☐ Veteran eligible to receive medications through the Veterans Health Administration, but chooses not to participate.
    - ☐ Veteran who does NOT have health insurance or has health insurance that does not pay for the drug prescribed.
- ✓ Ineligible for enrollment in Arizona Health Care Cost Containment System (AHCCCS; i.e. Arizona Medicaid).
- ✓ Medicare eligible, but NOT eligible for a full low-income subsidy.

PHARMACY LAW SIMPLIFIED

OTC SALE OF METHAMPHETAMINE PRECURSORS
ARS § 32-1977

- ✓ Over-the-counter (OTC) pseudoephedrine and ephedrine products must be kept behind the counter or in a locked cabinet away from customers.

PHOTO ID REQUIREMENT

The customer must present a valid government-issued photo ID at the point of sale.

DAILY & MONTHLY PURCHASE LIMITS FOR CUSTOMERS
- ✓ 3.6 grams/day per customer.
- ✓ 9 grams/month (30 days) per customer.

RECORDKEEPING REQUIREMENTS FOR RETAILERS
- ✓ Name and address of purchaser.
- ✓ Name and quantity of product sold.
- ✓ Date and time of sale.
- ✓ Type of photo ID presented by customer and the ID number printed on the ID.

ELECTRONIC SALES TRACKING SYSTEM REQUIREMENTS
- ✓ The retailer must use an electronic sales tracking system. Prior to each sale of ephedrine or pseudoephedrine, the retailer must submit the information recorded from each transaction (outlined above) electronically to the National Precursor Log Exchange (NPLEx).

- ✓ The system must be capable of generating "stop sale alerts" that prevent the retailer from completing the sale if the transaction will cause the customer to exceed daily and/or monthly purchase limits.

- ✓ The system must have an override function to override stop sale alerts when there is reasonable fear of bodily harm if the sale is not completed. The system must log each instance where an override is used.

- ✓ If a retailer does not have access to the electronic reporting system, the retailer must maintain a written log or some other type of electronic recordkeeping system.

RESTRICTIONS ARE LIMITED TO OVER-THE-COUNTER TRANSACTIONS

The limitations and requirements outlined above do NOT apply to ephedrine or pseudoephedrine obtained pursuant to a valid prescription.

OTC SALE OF DEXTROMETHORPHAN
ARS § 32-1978

- ✓ Purchaser must be at least 18 years of age.
- ✓ Retailer must require purchaser to provide proof of age, unless he/she appears to be at least 25 years-old.
- ✓ These requirements do not apply when dextromethorphan is obtained pursuant to a valid prescription.

POISONS AND HAZARDOUS SUBSTANCES
ARS § 32-1972

The label of a poison or hazardous substance must contain:
- ✓ Name and address of the manufacturer or seller.
- ✓ Common/usual name or chemical name of the substance.
- ✓ Depending on the properties of the substance, one (1) of the following signal words:
  - ⇨ "POISON" for poisons or highly toxic hazardous substances.
  - ⇨ "DANGER" for corrosive substances.
  - ⇨ "WARNING" or "caution" for any other types of poisons or hazardous substances.
- ✓ A statement that describes the poisonous property or some other major characteristic of the poison or hazardous substance. Examples include:
  - ⇨ "FLAMMABLE."
  - ⇨ "VAPOR HARMFUL."
  - ⇨ "CAUSES BURNS."
  - ⇨ "ABSORBED THROUGH SKIN."
- ✓ Precautionary measures.
- ✓ Instruction for first-aid (if necessary).
- ✓ Special handling and/or storage instructions.
- ✓ The statement "KEEP OUT OF REACH OF CHILDREN."
- ✓ Directions for use.

Note: If this information is not displayed prominently and conspicuously on the label in English, then the poison or hazardous substance is considered to be "misbranded."

CONTROLLED SUBSTANCES
SELECT EXAMPLES
ARS § 36-2501

SCHEDULE I CONTROLLED SUBSTANCES

Cannabis*	LSD	Peyote
GHB**	Mescaline	Psilocybin
Heroin	MDMA	

EXCEPTIONS:
* Marinol® is a C-III synthetic version of delta-9-tetrahydrocannabinol for nausea/vomiting and appetite stimulation.
** Xyrem® is a C-III version of GHB for narcolepsy available only through the Xyrem® REMS program.

SCHEDULE II CONTROLLED SUBSTANCES

C-II OPIOIDS
Alfentanil (Alfenta®)
Codeine
Diphenoxylate
Fentanyl (Duragesic®, Sublimaze®)
Hydrocodone (Lortab®, Norco®, Vicodin®, Tussionex®, Hycodan®, Hydromet®)
Hydromorphone (Dilaudid®, Exalgo®)
Methadone (Methadose®)
Morphine (Kadian®, MS Contin®, Roxanol®)
Opium (raw, extract, powdered, granulated, tincture of opium)
Oxycodone (Roxicodone®, Oxycontin®, Percocet®, Endocet®)
Oxymorphone (Opana®)
Sufentanil (Sufenta®)
Tapentadol (Nucynta®)

C-II STIMULANTS
Amphetamine/Dextroamphetamine (Adderall®)
Dextroamphetamine (Dexedrine®)
Lisdexamfetamine (Vyvanse®)
Methamphetamine (Desoxyn®)
Cocaine
Methylphenidate (Ritalin®, Daytrana®)
Methylphenidate Extended-Release (Concerta®)
Dexmethylphenidate (Focalin®)
Phenylacetone (immediate precursor to amphetamine and methamphetamine)

C-II DEPRESSANTS
Amobarbital (Amytal®)
Pentobarbital (Nembutal®)
Secobarbital (Seconal®)
Phencyclidine (PCP)

C-II HALLUCINOGENIC SUBSTANCE
Nabilone (Cesamet®)

SCHEDULE III CONTROLLED SUBSTANCES

C-III OPIOIDS
Paregoric
Codeine *
Morphine *
Opium *

* In low doses when supplied as a combination drug. For instance, codeine alone is a C-II opioid (technically an opiate, since derived without chemical modification from the opium poppy); however, when supplied in limited quantities in combination with acetaminophen it is sold as the C-III pain reliever known as Tylenol® #3.

C-III OPIOID PARTIAL AGONIST
Buprenorphine (Subutex®, Buprenex®, Suboxone®)

C-III MIXED OPIOID AGONIST/ANTAGONIST
Nalorphine (Lethodrone®, Nalline®)

C-III STIMULANTS
Benzphetamine (Didrex®, Regimex®)
Clortermine (Voranil®)
Phendimetrazine (Bontril®)

C-III DEPRESSANTS
Barbituric acid and derivatives
Sodium oxybate (Xyrem®)
Ketamine

THESE THREE (3) SCHEDULE II DEPRESSANTS ARE CATEGORIZED AS SCHEDULE III WHEN PART OF A COMPOUND, MIXTURE, OR SUPPOSITORY:

- ✓ Amobarbital
- ✓ Pentobarbital
- ✓ Secobarbital

C-III ANABOLIC STEROIDS
Boldenone (Equipoise®)
Methandrostenolone (Dianabol®)
Nandrolone (Durabolin®)
Oxandrolone (Oxandrin®)
Oxymetholone (Anadrol®)
Stanozolol (Winstrol®)
Testosterone (Androderm®, AndroGel®, Depo®-Testosterone, Testim®)

ALL ANABOLIC STEROIDS ARE SCHEDULE III CONTROLLED SUBSTANCES.

C-III HALLUCINOGENIC SUBSTANCE
Dronabinol (Marinol®)

SCHEDULE IV CONTROLLED SUBSTANCES

C-IV DEPRESSANTS (BENZODIAZEPINES)
Alprazolam (Xanax®)
Chlordiazepoxide (Librium®)
Clobazam (Onfi®)
Clonazepam (Klonopin®)
Clorazepate (Tranxene®)
Diazepam (Valium®)
Estazolam (Prosom®)
Flunitrazepam (Rohypnol®)
Flurazepam (Dalmane®)
Lorazepam (Ativan®)
Midazolam (Versed®)
Oxazepam (Serax®)
Temazepam (Restoril®)
Triazolam (Halcion®)

BENZODIAZEPINE DRUG NAME STEMS

All benzodiazepines are Schedule IV controlled substances. With few exceptions, the generic names of benzodiazepines contain the drug name stem "–azepam" or "–azolam."

C-IV DEPRESSANTS (NON-BENZODIAZEPINE)
Eszopiclone (Lunesta®)
Zaleplon (Sonata®)
Zolpidem (Ambien®)

C-IV DEPRESSANTS (SEDATIVE-HYPNOTICS AND ANXIOLYTICS)
Chloral hydrate (Somnote®)

C-IV DEPRESSANTS (BARBITURATES)
Barbital (Veronal®)
Phenobarbital (Luminal®)

C-IV MUSCLE RELAXANTS
Carisoprodol (Soma®)

C-IV OPIOIDS
Tramadol (Ultram®)

C-IV MIXED OPIOID AGONIST/ANTAGONISTS
Butorphanol (Stadol®)
Pentazocine (Talwin®)

C-IV STIMULANTS
Modafinil (Provigil®)
Phentermine (Adipex-P®)
Sibutramine (Meridia®)

C-IV WEIGHT-LOSS DRUGS
Lorcaserin (Belviq®)

SCHEDULE V CONTROLLED SUBSTANCES

C-V OPIOIDS
Codeine *
Diphenoxylate with atropine *

* In low doses when supplied as a combination drug. For example, codeine alone is a C-II opioid; however, when supplied in limited quantities in combination with guaifenesin, it is sold as a C-V cough suppressant (Robitussin® AC). Likewise, diphenoxylate is typically a C-II opioid; however, when supplied in limited quantities in combination with atropine, it is sold as a C-V anti-diarrheal medication (Lomotil®).

C-V DEPRESSANTS
Lacosamide (Vimpat®)
Pregabalin (Lyrica®)

C-V STIMULANTS
Pyrovalerone
Ephedrine

CONTROLLED SUBSTANCES CHARACTERIZED BY SCHEDULE

	Rx	OTC	ABUSE & DEPENDENCE	EXAMPLE
SCHEDULE I (C-I)			HIGH	HEROIN
SCHEDULE II (C-II)	✓		HIGH	ROXICODONE® OXYCODONE
SCHEDULE III (C-III)	✓		MODERATE	ANDROGEL® TESTOSTERONE
SCHEDULE IV (C-IV)	✓		MILD	VALIUM® DIAZEPAM
SCHEDULE V (C-V)	✓	✓	LOW	CHERATUSSIN® AC GUAIFENESIN WITH CODEINE

MANUFACTURE, DISTRIBUTION, AND DISPENSING OF CONTROLLED SUBSTANCES

ARS § 36-2522

A current Board-issued license or permit is required to manufacture, distribute, dispense, or prescribe any controlled substance in Arizona. Registration with Drug Enforcement Administration (DEA) is also required.

The following are NOT required to register with the DEA to handle controlled substances:
- ✓ Employees of a manufacturer, warehouse, distributor, or dispenser.
- ✓ Patients who obtain controlled substances legally (e.g. pursuant to a valid prescription).
- ✓ Government-employed officers or employees lawfully performing their duties.

CONTROLLED SUBSTANCE DISTRIBUTION

ARS § 36-2524

Schedule I and II controlled substances must only be distributed between people/entities registered with the DEA. Furthermore, transactions must be documented using a DEA Form 222.

PHARMACY CONTROLLED SUBSTANCE INVENTORY REQUIREMENTS

ARS § 36-2523

ARIZONA'S ANNUAL CONTROLLED SUBSTANCE INVENTORY REQUIREMENT

Pharmacies must take an inventory of Schedule II, III, IV, and V controlled substances EACH YEAR ON MAY 1ST or as directed by the Board.

In addition to the annual controlled substance inventory, an inventory of controlled substances must be taken in each of the following situations:
- ✓ When there is a change in the ownership of the pharmacy.
- ✓ When the pharmacy is discontinued/permanently closed.
- ✓ Within 10 days of a change in the pharmacist-in-charge.

All controlled substance records and inventories must be kept open for inspection by Arizona peace officers.

PHARMACY LAW
SIMPLIFIED

ARIZONA CONTROLLED SUBSTANCE LAW
ARS § 36-2525

CONTROLLED SUBSTANCE PRESCRIPTION LABELS
In addition to the label requirements outlined in ARS § 32-1968 (see page 41), controlled substance prescription labels must also include the name, address, and DEA number of the prescriber.

CANNOT PRESCRIBE MULTIPLE MEDICATIONS ON A SCHEDULE II PRESCRIPTION FORM

Prescription orders for Schedule II drugs can only contain one drug order per prescription blank. *

* Does not apply to hospital inpatient medication orders.

CHANGES TO SCHEDULE II PRESCRIPTIONS
With verbal authorization from the prescribing practitioner, a pharmacist has the authority to change any of the following information on a Schedule II prescription order:
- ✓ Date written.
- ✓ Strength.
- ✓ Dosage form.
- ✓ Quantity.
- ✓ Directions for use.

Note: Changes and the time and date of verbal authorization must be documented on the original prescription.

RECORDKEEPING REQUIREMENTS
SCHEDULE II PRESCRIPTION ORDERS
- ✓ Must be maintained in a file separate from all other prescription records.

SCHEDULE III, IV, AND V PRESCRIPTION ORDERS
- ✓ Maintain in a file separate from all other prescription records.

OR

- ✓ Maintain by marking the lower right corner of each prescription with the letter "C" using a font at least 1-inch-high with red ink and file with the non-controlled substance prescription records.

⇧
Requirement waived for pharmacies using an electronic recordkeeping system, as long as the system is capable of identifying prescriptions by serial number ("Rx number") and the original records can be retrieved using the prescriber's name, patient's name, drug dispensed, and date filled.

C-II PRESCRIPTION EXPIRATION

A Schedule II controlled substance prescription CANNOT be filled more than 90 days after the date issued.

EMERGENCY SCHEDULE II PRESCRIPTIONS

Emergency quantities of a Schedule II controlled substance may be dispensed pursuant to an oral prescription order (i.e. telephone authorization) communicated directly by the practitioner to the pharmacist.
- ⇨ The oral order must be reduced to writing immediately by the pharmacist.
- ⇨ The prescriber must supply the pharmacist with a written, manually signed prescription for the emergency supply dispensed within seven (7) days. The words "authorization for emergency dispensing" must be written on the face of this prescription.
- ⇨ If the pharmacist does not receive the written, manually signed prescription within 7 days, he/she must notify the Board. A pharmacist who fails to notify the board will lose his/her authority to dispense emergency Schedule II prescriptions pursuant to an oral order.

FAXED SCHEDULE II PRESCRIPTIONS

Generally, facsimile (faxed) Schedule II controlled substance prescriptions cannot be dispensed; however, there are three (3) exceptions which are outlined below.
- ⇨ C-II prescriptions to be compounded for direct injection or infusion.
- ⇨ C-II prescriptions for long-term care facility (LTCF) residents.
- ⇨ C-II prescriptions for patients enrolled in a hospice care program. *

* The prescribing practitioner or his/her agent must note "hospice patient" on the prescription prior to faxing.

In any of the three (3) special cases outlined above, the faxed C-II prescription order can serve as the original prescription order for recordkeeping purposes.

CONTROLLED SUBSTANCE REFILL LIMITS

- ✓ Schedule II controlled substance prescriptions CANNOT be refilled.

- ✓ Schedule III and IV controlled substance prescriptions and any associated refills may be filled within 6 months of the date issued. No more than 5 refills may be issued for each prescription. Additional quantities beyond 5 refills can only be dispensed if the prescriber issues a new and separate prescription order.

- ✓ Schedule V controlled substance prescriptions and any associated refills may be filled for one (1) year from the date issued. These prescriptions may be refilled as authorized. There are no official limits on the number of refills that can be issued.

OVER-THE-COUNTER CONTROLLED SUBSTANCE DISPENSING

- ✓ Customer must be at least 18 years of age.
- ✓ Must require identification (with proof of age, if necessary) from every unknown purchaser.
- ✓ Must be for a legitimate medical purpose.
- ✓ Must be dispensed by a pharmacist, pharmacy intern, or graduate intern. *
- ✓ Amount of medication dispensed to one person in a 48-hour period cannot exceed the following limits…
    - ⇨ 8 ounces (240 mL) of an opium-containing liquid drug product.
    - ⇨ 4 ounces (120 mL) of a liquid that contains a controlled substance other than opium.
    - ⇨ 48 dosage units of an opium-containing solid drug product.
    - ⇨ 24 dosage units of a solid drug product that contains a controlled substance other than opium.

* If dispensed by an intern, must be done so under the direct supervision of a pharmacist.

EPHEDRINE IS CLASSIFIED AS A SCHEDULE V CONTROLLED SUBSTANCE

According to the controlled substance law in Arizona, products that contain ephedrine as the single active ingredient are listed as Schedule V controlled substances. For these products, the over-the-counter purchase limit is 100 DOSAGE UNITS PER PERSON IN ANY 30-DAY PERIOD.

RECORDKEEPING REQUIREMENTS FOR CONTROLLED SUBSTANCES DISPENSED OTC

This information must be recorded for each OTC sale of a Schedule V controlled substance:
- ✓ Name and address of purchaser.
- ✓ Name and quantity of controlled substance purchased.
- ✓ Date of purchase.
- ✓ Name or initials of dispensing pharmacist or intern.

Note: Per federal law, all controlled substance records must be maintained for at least 2 years.

LABEL REQUIREMENTS FOR CONTROLLED SUBSTANCES DISPENSED OTC

Information required to appear on the container of a controlled substance directly dispensed by a practitioner or pharmacist, but not for immediate administration (e.g. not for a hospital inpatient):
- ✓ Name and address of dispensing practitioner or pharmacist.
- ✓ Serial number (i.e. "Rx number").
- ✓ Date of dispensing.
- ✓ Name of prescriber.
- ✓ Name of patient. *
- ✓ Directions for use.
- ✓ Cautionary statements from the prescription order or as required by law (if any).
- ✓ For Schedule II, III, and IV controlled substances, a warning such as "Caution: federal law prohibits the transfer of this drug to any person other than the patient for whom it was prescribed."

* For animals, the name of the owner and the species of the animal.

E-PRESCRIBING CONTROLLED SUBSTANCES

Schedule II, III, IV, and V controlled substance prescriptions may be transmitted electronically (i.e. via e-prescription) from the prescribing practitioner to the pharmacy.

PHARMACY LAW SIMPLIFIED

CONTROLLED SUBSTANCES PRESCRIPTION MONITORING PROGRAM

ARS § 36-2603, ARS § 36-2604, ARS § 36-2608, ARS § 36-2610, R4-23-501, R4-23-502, & R4-23-503

CONTROLLED SUBSTANCES PRESCRIPTION MONITORING PROGRAM (CSPMP)
- ⇨ Provides a computerized central database tracking system that tracks prescribing, dispensing, and consumption of Schedule II, III, and IV controlled substances.
- ⇨ Assists law enforcement in identifying illegal activities related to controlled substance prescriptions.
- ⇨ Provides information to help avoid inappropriate use of controlled substances.

CSPMP REGISTRATION REQUIREMENTS
- ✓ Licensed medical practitioners that possess a current DEA registration must be registered in the CSPMP.
- ✓ For pharmacists to access the CSPMP, they must have a current pharmacist license, complete the CSPMP Online Training Program offered by the Board, and request access from the CSPMP Director.

CSPMP REPORTING REQUIREMENTS
Medical practitioners, health care facilities, and pharmacies that prescribe or dispense Schedule II, III, or IV controlled substance prescriptions* in Arizona must report this information to the CSPMP:
- ✓ Pharmacy's name, address, phone number, and DEA registration number.
- ✓ Patient's name, address, phone number, date of birth, and gender (for animals, use owner's information).
- ✓ Prescriber's name, address, phone number, and DEA registration number.
- ✓ Name, strength, quantity, dose, and NDC number of the controlled substance dispensed.
- ✓ Rx number.
- ✓ Date written and date of dispensing.
- ✓ Whether the prescription is new or a refill.
- ✓ Number of refills authorized by the prescriber (if any).
- ✓ Method of payment (i.e. cash or third party).

Notice that C-V prescription information is not reported to the CSPMP.

Pharmacies must report C-II, C-III, and C-IV dispensing records (as outlined above) from the previous week (Sunday through Saturday) electronically by close of business each Friday. If the Friday for a particular week happens to be a state holiday, then the deadline is moved to the next business day.

DRUGS EXEMPT FROM CSPMP REPORTING REQUIREMENTS
- ✓ Drug samples.
- ✓ Drugs administered directly to the patient.
- ✓ Drugs issued through narcotic treatment programs.
- ✓ Drugs dispensed in limited quantities by a practitioner within a health care facility.
    - ⇨ No more than a 72-hour supply and not more than twice within 15 days.

USE AND RELEASE OF CONFIDENTIAL INFORMATION
Prescription information submitted to the Board via the CSPMP is confidential and is not public record; however, the Board may release information collected by the CSPMP as follows:
- ✓ To an individual requesting his/her own information.
- ✓ To a prescriber or dispenser (or a delegated healthcare professional) for evaluation of a patient.
- ✓ To a medical regulatory board, law enforcement, criminal justice agency, county medical examiner, forensic pathologist, or the AHCCCS* for an open investigation or complaint.
- ✓ To a person serving a lawful court order.
- ✓ To entities for statistical, research, or educational use, but only after removing patient information.

Arizona Health Care Cost Containment System

Note: Disclosing information from the CSPMP for illegitimate purposes is a felony.

COMPUTER RECORDS
R4-23-408

RESPONSIBILITIES OF THE PHARMACY PERMITTEE OR PHARMACIST-IN-CHARGE
- Preparing and implementing policies and procedures for computer use in the pharmacy.
    - Procedures to follow when the computer system is not operational.
    - Procedures for routine backup of data.
    - Audit procedures.
    - Assignment of personnel codes.
    - Data entry quality assurance procedures.
- Notifying the DEA and the Board in writing that prescription files are being stored in a pharmacy computer system.
- Ensuring that one (1) of the following two methods are used to document the accuracy of original and refill prescription information...
    - Hardcopy printout of daily original and refill prescription data.
        - Must state that prescription data is reviewed by a pharmacist for accuracy.
        - Includes printed name of each dispensing pharmacist.
        - Must be signed and initialed by each dispensing pharmacist.
    - Log book or separate file of daily statements.
        - Must state that prescription data is reviewed by a pharmacist for accuracy.
        - Includes printed name of each dispensing pharmacist.
        - Must be signed and initialed by each dispensing pharmacist.
- Ensuring that the computer system has the necessary safeguards and security features.

ELECTRONIC RECORDKEEPING REQUIREMENTS
For prescription files that are stored in an electronic imaging recordkeeping system, the system must...
- Capture an exact image of the prescription (including the back, if necessary).
- Include any notes of clarification or alterations that are directly associated with the image.
- Store the image and associated notes for at least seven (7) years from the date of last dispensing.
- The original hardcopy (if applicable) must be kept for at least 30 days after the date dispensed. *

* **EXCEPTION:** Schedule II prescriptions – all original C-II prescription orders must be kept for at least seven (7) years after the date dispensed. An electronic image cannot serve as the original prescription order for recordkeeping purposes.

CURRENT GOOD COMPOUNDING PRACTICES
R4-23-410

All ingredients used in compounding must meet official compendium requirements (i.e. USP and National Formulary), be of high quality, and be obtained from an acceptable and reliable source according to the pharmacist's professional judgement.

An established prescribing pattern MUST exist before a pharmacist compounds a product in excess of the quantity to be dispensed in anticipation of receiving valid prescriptions for the product.

Compounding products for other pharmacies, practitioners, or for distribution is prohibited. The exception is compounding a product for a practitioner to administer to his/her patients; however, the product must be accompanied by a written list of active ingredients and the label must include:
- ✓ Pharmacy's name, address, and phone number.
- ✓ Name of the compounded product and some indication that that product was compounded.
- ✓ Lot number or control number.
- ✓ Beyond-use-date (BUD).
- ✓ The following statements:
    - ⇨ "Not for Dispensing"
    - ⇨ "For Office or Hospital Administration Only"

THE ADVERTISING OF COMPOUNDING SERVICES IS PERMITTED.

Pharmacists are responsible for the following aspects of compounding:
- ✓ Approval or rejection of ingredients, containers/lids, and labeling.
- ✓ Preparation of compounding records.
- ✓ Reviewing records to ensure the compounding process is error-free.
- ✓ Ensuring that compounding equipment is properly used, maintained, and cleaned.
- ✓ Initialing or signing the compounding record to indicate fulfillment of these responsibilities.

COMPOUNDING RECORDS MUST BE KEPT FOR AT LEAST SEVEN (7) YEARS.

Pharmacists must also...
- ✓ Comply with current good compounding practices.
- ✓ Maintain proficiency in compounding (e.g. training and CE).
- ✓ Ensure that compounding personnel wear clean clothes and protective apparel (gloves, face mask, etc.).

Compounding personnel who are sick or have a lesion/wound that could come into contact with the components, container, or label of a compounded product MUST BE EXCLUDED from compounding.

The compounding area must have enough space for efficient activity, free movement, and visual surveillance by a pharmacist. It must also have a clean, dry, temperature-controlled area (with a refrigerator, if necessary) to store bulk drugs and materials used in compounding.

Compounding equipment and utensils must be clean, non-porous, and compatible with compounding ingredients. Equipment must be calibrated routinely to ensure proper performance.

Procedures must be in place to PREVENT CROSS-CONTAMINATION by products that require special precautions (e.g. penicillin).

Documentation for each compounded drug product must include...
- ✓ The identity of ingredients used (including the manufacturer, lot number, and expiration date).
- ✓ The order in which the ingredients were combined and how the product was compounded.
- ✓ The equipment, utensils, and containers/lids used.

Note: Records must be kept for seven (7) years.

Compounding procedures must include assessment of processes that may lead to variations in the quantity or quality of the final compounded product.

The pharmacist is responsible for checking and re-checking each stage of the compounding process.

The pharmacist must sign/initial documentation indicating the compounding process is complete and accurate.

In addition to the information required to appear on a standard prescription label (outlined below), labels for compounded prescriptions must also include:
- ✓ Symbol, statement, or abbreviation that indicates the product was compounded.
- ✓ Beyond-use-date (BUD).

INFORMATION THAT MUST APPEAR ON A STANDARD PRESCRIPTION LABEL
ARS § 32-1968

- ✓ Pharmacy's name and address.
- ✓ Serial number ("Rx number").
- ✓ Date of dispensing.
- ✓ Prescriber's name.
- ✓ Patient's name (for animals, the owner's name and the species of the animal).
- ✓ Directions for use.
- ✓ Any cautionary statements contained in the order.

When an ingredient is transferred from its original container to a different container, the new container must be labeled with the following information (may be printed on the label using an abbreviated code system):
- ✓ Name of the ingredient.
- ✓ Name of the manufacturer or supplier.
- ✓ Lot number.
- ✓ Weight or volume.
- ✓ Beyond-use-date (BUD).
- ✓ Date of transfer.

When quantities of a compounded product (in excess of what was dispensed) are stored in a pharmacy, the container label must include the following information:
- ✓ A complete list of ingredients (or the name of the final product).
- ✓ Date prepared.
- ✓ Lot number. *
- ✓ Beyond-use-date. *

* Assigned by the pharmacy.

IMPRINT CODE REQUIREMENT FOR LEGEND DRUGS
ARS § 32-1975

- ✓ "Legend drugs" are prescription only ("Rx-only") drugs.

- ✓ Any legend drug that is a solid oral dosage form (e.g. oral capsule or tablet) manufactured or distributed in Arizona must have a clear and prominent imprinted code that can be used to identify the drug product and the manufacturer.

- ✓ The "imprinted code" must be a series of numbers and/or letters +/- marks or monograms that are unique to the manufacturer or distributor.

CONGRUENCE WITH FEDERAL REGULATIONS

21 CFR § 206.10 imposes a similar requirement for imprinted codes on Rx-only solid oral dosage forms.

- ✓ If a particular solid oral dosage form has some unique characteristic(s) that preclude the use of an imprinted code, a manufacturer can request an exemption from the Board.

- ✓ Solid oral dosage forms compounded by a pharmacist are exempt from the imprint requirement.

PHARMACY LAW
SIMPLIFIED

COMMUNITY PHARMACY
SPACE AND BARRIER REQUIREMENTS
R4-23-609

MINIMUM SPACE REQUIREMENT
The minimum space requirement for the pharmacy area (i.e. the area designated for stocking, compounding, and dispensing drugs) in a community pharmacy must be AT LEAST 300 SQUARE FEET to accommodate up to three (3) employees + 60 square feet of floor area for each additional employee working at the same time.

The entire space must permit free movement and visual surveillance by the pharmacist.

The compounding and dispensing counter must provide at least 3 square feet of space per working licensee. *
Each 3 square foot section must be at least 16 inches deep and 24 inches long.

* Includes pharmacists, graduate interns, pharmacy interns, pharmacy technicians, and pharmacy technician trainees.

The floor near the working space of the counter (where the employees stand) must be clear and continuous for at least 36 inches (i.e. no structures blocking the space).

DESIGNATED SPACE FOR PATIENT COUNSELING
Each pharmacy that dispenses drugs/devices to outpatients must have a separate and distinct area for patient counseling to provide privacy.

STORAGE OF CONTROLLED SUBSTANCES IN A COMMUNITY PHARMACY SETTING

Community pharmacies may store controlled substances by one of these two (2) methods:
- ✓ In a locked cabinet or safe.
- ✓ Dispersed throughout the pharmacy's stock of prescription-only drugs.

PHYSICAL BARRIER REQUIREMENTS
The pharmacy area must be enclosed by a permanent partition/barrier constructed of material that cannot be easily removed, penetrated, or bent. The barrier must extend from the floor or counter to the ceiling or roof. If the barrier is made of material with openings, the openings cannot be large enough to allow removal of items from the pharmacy area.

While open for business, the ~~pharmacy area~~ working counter area must be protected from unauthorized access by a barrier at least 66 inches high or by some other Board-approved method.

Doors to the pharmacy area must be securely locking.

DRUG STORAGE
Storage conditions in the pharmacy area must comply with drug package labeling or an official compendium. Generally, the storage area must be dry, well-lighted, ventilated, clean, and orderly.

If additional storage areas (outside of the pharmacy area) are required, then access to these areas must be limited to pharmacists only, except in extreme emergencies. *

* Extreme emergencies include FIRE, WATER LEAK, ELECTRICAL FAILURE, PUBLIC DISASTER, or some other catastrophe that constitutes an imminent threat of physical harm to pharmacy personnel or patrons. R4-23-110

COMMUNITY PHARMACY
PERSONNEL AND SECURITY PROCEDURES
R4-23-610

- ✓ Every pharmacy must have a person designated as the pharmacist-in-charge.

RESPONSIBILITIES OF THE PHARMACIST-IN-CHARGE
- ✓ Ensuring preparation, implementation, and compliance with pharmacy policies and procedures.
- ✓ Reviewing and, if necessary, making changes to policies and procedures biennially (every 2 years).
- ✓ Assembling policies and procedures into a written or electronic manual.
- ✓ Making the manual available in the pharmacy for employee reference and Board inspection.

The pharmacist-in-charge must also ensure that the number of personnel working in the pharmacy is compliant with the space per licensee requirement (300 square feet for the first three (3) workers and an additional 60 squarer feet for each additional person working at the same time; plus, the counter space requirement of three (3) square feet per licensee).

PERSONNEL ALLOWED IN THE PHARMACY AREA
- ✓ Pharmacists.
- ✓ Graduate and pharmacy interns.
- ✓ Pharmacy technicians and pharmacy technician trainees.
- ✓ Support personnel (e.g. cashiers).
- ✓ Compliance officers.
- ✓ Drug inspectors.
- ✓ Peace officers (acting in an official capacity).
- ✓ Other designated personnel and persons authorized by law.

Pharmacy personnel (e.g. interns, technicians) are only permitted to be in the pharmacy area when a pharmacist is present, except in extreme emergencies. *

> * Extreme emergencies include FIRE, WATER LEAK, ELECTRICAL FAILURE, PUBLIC DISASTER, or some other catastrophe that constitutes an imminent threat of physical harm to pharmacy personnel or patrons. [R4-23-110]

OTHER KEY POINTS
- ✓ The pharmacist on duty must ensure the pharmacy is physically secure from unauthorized access.

- ✓ The pharmacy permittee or pharmacist-in-charge must ensure that drugs received outside of the pharmacy area are immediately transferred unopened into the pharmacy area. Only a pharmacist or pharmacy personnel under supervision of a pharmacist can open a drug shipment.

- ✓ The pharmacy permittee or pharmacist-in-charge may provide a small slot/opening to accept new prescription orders or refill requests when the pharmacist is not present.

PHARMACY FACILITY REQUIREMENTS
R4-23-611

- ✓ The pharmacy must have trash cans that are emptied periodically throughout the day.

- ✓ The pharmacy must have toilet facilities that are clean and in good repair.
  - ⇨ Within 100 feet walking distance (or other Board-approved distance) from the pharmacy area. *
    - May be located within the pharmacy area.

  * Distance requirement applies if permit was issued or pharmacy was remodeled after 2/1/2014.

- ✓ The pharmacy must have a sink with hot and cold running water for preparing drug products.

- ✓ Pharmacy personnel and their apparel must be clean while in the pharmacy area.

- ✓ No animals are permitted in the pharmacy, except licensed assistance animals and guard animals.

- ✓ The pharmacy must be free of insects and rodents.

- ✓ A supply of chemicals sufficient to meet demand must be kept on-hand.

PHARMACY EQUIPMENT REQUIREMENTS
R4-23-612

The pharmacy permittee or pharmacist-in-charge must ensure that the pharmacy has...
- ✓ Refrigerators dedicated to the storage of drugs.
- ✓ A record of over-the-counter controlled substance sales (if applicable).
- ✓ Graduates in various sizes (for measuring liquids).
- ✓ Spatulas in various sizes, one of which must be non-metallic.
- ✓ One mortar and pestle. *
- ✓ A class A prescription balance with weights or an electronic balance with equal or greater accuracy. *
- ✓ One ointment tile or equivalent (e.g. glass ointment slab). *
- ✓ Current copy of Arizona Pharmacy Act, administrative rules, and Arizona Controlled Substances Act. **
- ✓ Professional reference library consisting of at least one reference or text on the following subjects: **
  - ⇨ Pharmacology or Toxicology
  - ⇨ Therapeutics
  - ⇨ Drug Compatibility
  - ⇨ Drug Product Equivalency
- ✓ Various labels (e.g. Rx labels and auxiliary labels).
- ✓ A stamp for the letter "C" in red ink at least one-inch-high if storing C-III, C-IV, and C-V prescription records in the same file with non-controlled substance prescription records.
- ✓ Current antidote and drug interaction information.
- ✓ Poison control phone number displayed in the pharmacy area.

* This equipment is not required if the permittee indicates in the application that the pharmacy will not be compounding.
** Physical or electronic.

AUTOMATED STORAGE AND DISTRIBUTION SYSTEMS

R4-23-614

A pharmacy permittee or pharmacist-in-charge of a pharmacy with automated storage and distribution systems that allow access BY PATIENTS must ensure that the system...
- ✓ Only contains prescriptions that DO NOT require consultation (i.e. refills).
- ✓ Only contains prescriptions that have been properly labeled and verified by a pharmacist.
- ✓ Allows the patient to choose whether or not use the system.
- ✓ Is located in the wall of the pharmacy or secured to a wall or floor within 20 feet of the pharmacy.
- ✓ Has a mechanism to identify the patient and release only the prescription(s) of the identified patient.
- ✓ Provides a mechanism through which the patient can obtain pharmacist consultation.
- ✓ Does not allow refills to be dispensed when the pharmacist deems that counseling is necessary.

A pharmacy permittee or pharmacist-in-charge of a pharmacy with automated storage and distribution systems that allow access ONLY BY LICENSED PERSONNEL must ensure that the system...
- ✓ Prevents unauthorized persons from accessing drugs/devices.
- ✓ Allows authorized licensed personnel access to fill, stock, or restock drugs/devices.

QUALITY ASSURANCE PROGRAM

Pharmacies must have an ongoing quality assurance program in place prior to using any automated storage and distribution system.

As with all other pharmacy policies and procedures, the policies and procedures related to a pharmacy automated dispensing system must be...
- ✓ Assembled into a manual (written or electronic).
- ✓ Made available for employee reference and Board inspection.
- ✓ Reviewed and, if necessary, changed/updated biennially (once every two (2) years).

Note: The Board may prohibit the use of automated storage and distribution systems for a pharmacy that fails to comply with the requirements of this section (R4-23-614).

MECHANICAL STORAGE AND COUNTING DEVICE FOR SOLID ORAL DOSAGE FORMS
R4-23-615

Each cell or cassette in a mechanical storage and counting device must have a label affixed to the front that displays the name and strength of the drug product stored therein.

The pharmacy must maintain a log (paper or electronic) that records the NDC number, expiration date, and lot number from the stock bottle(s) used to fill each cell/cassette. The date the cell/cassette is filled, the identity of the licensee filling the cell/cassette, and the identity of the supervising pharmacist must also be logged.

The paper or electronic log must be kept available for Board inspection for at least two (2) years.

To ensure the accuracy of the device, the pharmacy permittee or pharmacist-in-charge must implement and document personnel training, maintenance, calibration, routine quality assurance, and accuracy validation testing.

As with all other pharmacy policies and procedures, the policies and procedures related to mechanical storage and counting devices for solid oral dosage forms must be…
- ✓ Assembled into a manual (written or electronic).
- ✓ Made available for employee reference and Board inspection.
- ✓ Reviewed and, if necessary, changed/updated biennially (once every two (2) years).

A COMMON REAL-WORLD SITUATION & WHAT YOU NEED TO KNOW

THE SITUATION
A drug has been counted by the mechanical storage and counting device, but has not left the pharmacy and needs to be returned to the cell/cassette.

WHAT YOU NEED TO KNOW
Drugs can only be returned to the cell/cassette using a Board-approved method that implements technology to prevent drug return errors.

Note: The Board may prohibit the use of mechanical storage and counting devices for a pharmacy that fails to comply with the requirements of this section (R4-23-615).

EXAMPLE OF A MECHANICAL STORAGE AND COUNTING DEVICE

ScriptPro® Robotic Dispensing System

MECHANICAL COUNTING DEVICE FOR SOLID ORAL DOSAGE FORMS
R4-23-616

To ensure the accuracy of the device, the pharmacy permittee or pharmacist-in-charge must implement and document personnel training, maintenance, calibration, routine quality assurance, and accuracy validation testing.

As with all other pharmacy policies and procedures, the policies and procedures related to mechanical counting devices for solid oral dosage forms must be...
- ✓ Assembled into a manual (written or electronic).
- ✓ Made available for employee reference and Board inspection.
- ✓ Reviewed and, if necessary, changed/updated biennially (once every two (2) years).

Note: The Board may prohibit the use of mechanical counting devices for a pharmacy that fails to comply with the requirements of this section (R4-23-616).

EXAMPLE OF A MECHANICAL COUNTING DEVICE

Kirby Lester KL1 Pharmacy Tablet Counter

TEMPORARY PHARMACY FACILITIES OR MOBILE PHARMACIES
R4-23-617

In declared disaster areas, if necessary, the following pharmacies may TEMPORARILY establish or relocate to a mobile/temporary pharmacy facility:
- ✓ Pharmacies within a declared disaster area.
- ✓ Non-resident pharmacies.
- ✓ Pharmacies permitted/licensed in another state/jurisdiction, but not licensed in Arizona.

The pharmacist-in-charge of a mobile/temporary pharmacy facility must ensure that...
- ✓ The pharmacy is under control and management of a supervising pharmacist/pharmacist-in-charge.
- ✓ The pharmacy is in or adjacent to the declared disaster area.
- ✓ The Board is notified of the location of the pharmacy.
- ✓ The pharmacy is properly secured.
- ✓ The pharmacy records are kept in compliance with Arizona statutes and rules.
- ✓ Pharmacy services STOP being provided when the state of emergency ends.

The Board has the authority to approve or deny, and to monitor and inspect mobile/temporary pharmacies.

SHARED SERVICES
R4-23-621

Examples of shared services include remote order entry and the filling of prescriptions by central fill pharmacies.

A pharmacy may use shared services if both pharmacies are owned by the same person/entity or if they enter into a contract or written agreement outlining the responsibilities of each party.

Pharmacies using shared services must share technology (e.g. a common electronic file) that allows access to information required to perform the shared service.

Before a pharmacy can use a shared service, patients must be notified that their prescriptions may be processed or filled by another pharmacy. Notification can be made via a one-time written notice or a sign in the pharmacy. The notification must identify the name of the pharmacy providing the shared service.

SPECIAL LABELING REQUIREMENT

If the prescription order is filled and delivered to the patient directly using a shared service, a statement to this effect must appear on the label of the container or on a paper accompanying the container:

"Written information about this prescription has been provided for you. Please read this information before you take the medication. If you have questions concerning this prescription, a pharmacist is available during normal business hours to answer these questions at [insert the local and toll-free telephone numbers of the pharmacy using the shared services]."

Patient notification of shared services is not required in facilities, such as hospitals, where medications are administered by licensed health care professionals.

Whenever providing or receiving shared services, each pharmacy must record the name, initials, or ID code of the person who took part in each step of processing a prescription.

Records must be provided within 72 hours upon request from the Board (or a designee of the Board).

Disciplinary action taken by another state's board of pharmacy (or equivalent) involving shared services must be reported to the Arizona Board of Pharmacy as soon as possible.

A pharmacy's electronic database can be accessed from inside or outside the pharmacy to perform order processing functions, as long as there are controls in place to protect the integrity and confidentiality of patient information and none of the information is copied or removed from the database.

HOSPITAL PHARMACIES
ARS § 32-1934

- ✓ Hospital pharmacies must obtain a permit from the Board just like all other types of pharmacies.
- ✓ Medications given to patients upon discharge must be properly labeled and dispensed by a pharmacist.
- ✓ The pharmacist-in-charge is responsible for procedures related to drug and device acquisition, stocking, recordkeeping, and dispensing.

PHARMACY SUPERVISION REQUIREMENTS BASED ON HOSPITAL SIZE

HOSPITALS WITH < 50 BEDS
The pharmacist is only required to supply services on a part-time basis upon written approval and recommendation from the Board, as long as prescription processing/dispensing activities do not take place when the pharmacist is absent.

HOSPITALS WITH ≥ 50 BEDS
The pharmacy must be under the continuous supervision of a pharmacist during the pharmacy's hours of operation.

OBTAINING DRUGS WHEN A PHARMACIST IS NOT PRESENT

Nurses may obtain emergency drugs from the hospital pharmacy in the absence of a pharmacist in accordance with procedures that are recommended and approved by the Board on a hospital-by-hospital basis.

HOSPITAL PHARMACY PERSONNEL
R4-23-653

Each hospital pharmacy must be directed by a licensed pharmacist (the "Director of Pharmacy").

The Director of Pharmacy may serve as the pharmacist-in-charge or appoint a pharmacist-in-charge.

The Director of Pharmacy (and pharmacist-in-charge) are responsible for all hospital pharmacy activities and must ensure policies and procedures following Arizona law are prepared, implemented, and complied with.

As with all other pharmacy policies and procedures, these policies and procedures must be...
- ✓ Assembled into a manual (written or electronic).
- ✓ Made available for employee reference and Board inspection.
- ✓ Reviewed and, if necessary, changed/updated biennially (once every two (2) years).

Hospital pharmacies must provide services at least 40 hours/week* and a pharmacist must be present in the hospital at all times when the pharmacy is open, except in extreme emergencies.
* Requirement may be reduced with written permission from the Board.

ON-CALL PHARMACIST

If the hospital pharmacy is open less than 24 hours/day, a pharmacist must be on-call to provide consultation, drug information services, and to review or dispense orders during the time the pharmacy is closed.

In a hospital pharmacy setting, the following tasks are considered to be "professional practice" and must be completed by a pharmacist (or a pharmacy intern or graduate intern under the supervision of a pharmacist):
- ✓ Verify medication orders for therapeutic and pharmaceutical feasibility based on...
    - ⇨ Medical condition.
    - ⇨ Allergies.
    - ⇨ Incompatibilities (medical and pharmaceutical).
    - ⇨ Recommended dosage limits.

    Note: Medication orders must be verified before patient administration, except in emergency medical situations or if the pharmacy was closed (non-24-hour pharmacy) in which case the order must be verified within four (4) hours of opening the pharmacy.
- ✓ Measure, count, pour, compound, admix, combine, or otherwise prepare and package drugs for dispensing.
    - ⇨ May be completed by a pharmacy technician or technician trainee under pharmacist supervision.
- ✓ Verify that tasks are performed correctly and yield safe and accurate results when performed by a pharmacy technician or pharmacy technician trainee.
- ✓ Supervise drug re-packaging and check the final re-packaged product.
- ✓ Supervise aseptic technique and drug incompatibility training and education.
- ✓ Consult with medical practitioners on drug therapy and medical conditions.
- ✓ When requested, or otherwise deemed necessary, provide patient consultations.
- ✓ Monitor drug therapy to ensure safe and effective outcomes.
- ✓ Provide drug information to patients and health care professionals.
- ✓ Manage pharmacy personnel and systems to ensure safety and accuracy.
- ✓ Verify accuracy of medication orders.
- ✓ Ensure compliance with the hospital pharmacy's quality assurance program.

The Director of Pharmacy and pharmacist-in-charge are responsible for supervising hospital pharmacy activities.

Pharmacists are responsible for supervising and ensuring the competence and safety of all activities performed by pharmacy technicians, pharmacy technician trainees, and other pharmacy personnel.

ABSENCE OF PHARMACIST
R4-23-654

A hospital pharmacy cannot be without a pharmacist for more than 72 consecutive hours.

If a pharmacist is not on duty, medical staff/authorized personnel must have access to a remote drug storage area and/or the hospital pharmacy.

The Director of Pharmacy or the pharmacist-in-charge must make arrangements to provide access to these areas prior to the pharmacist's absence.

Additionally, when a pharmacist is not on duty, medical staff/authorized personnel must have access to an on-call pharmacist by telephone.

The Director of Pharmacy or pharmacist-in-charge AND a committee of the hospital are responsible for working together to decide which medications will be stocked in the remote drug storage area.

Authority to access the hospital pharmacy when it is closed is delegated to one (1) supervisory nurse per shift.

This nurse must have special training on procedures for pharmacy access, drug removal, and recordkeeping.

Conditions that must exist for the authorized nurse to enter the pharmacy:
1) The pharmacy is closed,
2) The drug is not available in the remote drug storage area, AND
3) The drug is needed to meet the immediate needs of a patient whose health may be compromised.

AUTHORITY CANNOT BE DELEGATED EXCEPT IN EMERGENCIES

The authorized nurse CAN DELEGATE the authority to enter the pharmacy to another nurse in an EMERGENCY; however, in normal situations the authority to enter the pharmacy cannot be delegated.

Information that must be recorded by the nurse when removing a drug from the pharmacy:
- ✓ Patient's name.
- ✓ Drug name, strength, and dosage form.
- ✓ Quantity removed.
- ✓ Date and time of removal.
- ✓ Nurse's signature or initials.

Note: The nurse must attach this information to the medication order (or a copy of the medication order) AND place the documentation (described above) in a conspicuous place in the pharmacy.

The pharmacist must verify the drug removal records) within four (4) hours of returning from an absence.

PHARMACY LAW
SIMPLIFIED

HOSPITAL PHARMACY SECURITY
R4-23-657

The Director of Pharmacy is responsible for the security of the pharmacy.

The pharmacy area must remain locked (by key or programmable code) to prevent unauthorized access.

With the following exceptions, no one is permitted to be in the pharmacy when the pharmacist is absent.
- ✓ An authorized nurse supervisor following procedures to remove a drug for the immediate need of a patient.
- ✓ If only one (1) pharmacist is on duty and must leave for an emergency or for patient care duties, then the other pharmacy personnel (e.g. interns and technicians) may remain in the pharmacy to work as long as the all C-II drugs are locked up and the pharmacist is available in the hospital.

All licensed pharmacy personnel must wear an ID badge with name and title/position while on duty.

HOSPITAL PHARMACY FACILITY REQUIREMENTS
R4-23-655

MINIMUM SPACE REQUIREMENT
At least 500 square feet must be dedicated to preparation and dispensing functions. *
Note: In certain circumstances, the Board may allow a pharmacy to be operated in a smaller space.
* This requirement only applies for permits issued or remodels done after 1/31/2003.

The Board may require additional space for pharmacies that prepare, dispense, or store investigational drugs, chemotherapy drugs, emergency drug kits, radiopharmaceuticals, etc.

PHYSICAL BARRIER REQUIREMENT
Hospital pharmacies must be enclosed by a permanent partition/barrier from floor to ceiling and equipped with securely locking doors.

DRUG STORAGE
Prior to dispensing, drugs must be stored in a locked area under pharmacist control, such inside the pharmacy.

The storage area must be clean, secure, and segregated, and provide a well-lighted, ventilated, moisture-controlled, temperature-controlled environment.

HOSPITAL PHARMACY EQUIPMENT
R4-23-656

HOSPITAL PHARMACY EQUIPMENT REQUIREMENTS
- ✓ A professional reference library (hardcopy or electronic) appropriate for the pharmacy services provided.
- ✓ A clean, functional sink with hot and cold running water used for preparing drugs.
- ✓ A refrigerator and freezer maintained at temperatures for proper drug storage.
- ✓ A designated area for a laminar airflow hood with supplies for preparing sterile drug products/infusions.
- ✓ Temperature controls to maintain an environment for proper drug storage.

PHARMACY LAW SIMPLIFIED

HOSPITAL DRUG DISTRIBUTION AND CONTROL
R4-23-658

The Director of Pharmacy must develop and implement policies and procedures for the…
- ✓ Secure distribution and control of prescription order blanks bearing identification of the hospital.
- ✓ Operation of a drug distribution system that optimizes patient safety. *

* May be developed and implemented by the pharmacist-in-charge.

The Director of Pharmacy is also responsible for…
- ✓ Safe and efficient procurement, dispensing, distribution, administration, and control of drugs.
- ✓ Consulting with personnel and medical staff committees to develop a formulary.
- ✓ Handling and distributing investigational drugs.
- ✓ Regular inspections of drug storage and preparation areas.

ACCEPTABLE MEDICATION ORDER FORMATS FOR HOSPITALS
- ✓ Original written order (or direct copy).
- ✓ Faxed copy of the original written order.
- ✓ Verbal order.

REQUIREMENT TO REVIEW ORDERS PRIOR TO ADMINISTRATION

Medication orders must be reviewed by a pharmacist before the initial dose is administered to the patient. *
* This rule does not apply in emergency medical situations or when the pharmacy is closed.

HOSPITAL PRESCRIPTION LABEL REQUIREMENTS
Drugs dispensed/distributed by a hospital pharmacy for use within the hospital must be labeled as follows:

SINGLE UNIT PACKAGES
- ✓ Drug name, strength, and dosage form.
- ✓ Lot number and beyond-use-date (BUD).
- ✓ Auxiliary label(s).

RE-PACKAGED PREPARATIONS
- ✓ Drug name, strength, and dosage form.
- ✓ Lot number and beyond-use-date (BUD).
- ✓ Auxiliary labels.
- ✓ Mechanism to identify the pharmacist responsible for re-packaging.

IV ADMIXTURE PREPARATIONS
- ✓ Patient's name and location.
- ✓ Name and quantity of base solution.
- ✓ Name and amount of drug added.
- ✓ Date prepared.
- ✓ Beyond-use-date and time.
- ✓ Administration guidelines.
- ✓ Auxiliary labels and precautionary statements.
- ✓ Initials of the pharmacist responsible for preparation.

The Director of Pharmacy or pharmacist-in-charge must ensure development, implementation, and compliance with policies and procedures for use, accountability, and recordkeeping of controlled substances in the hospital.

Emergency departments may dispense drugs when the pharmacy is unable to do so. If emergency department dispensing takes place, policies and procedures must ensure that...
- ✓ Drugs are only dispensed to patients admitted to the emergency department.
- ✓ Drugs are only dispensed by an authorized medical practitioner (not a designee or agent of the provider).
- ✓ Drugs available for dispensing are designed to meet the immediate need of the patient.
- ✓ Dispensed quantities are limited to meet patient need until outpatient pharmacy services are available.
- ✓ Drugs are pre-packaged by a pharmacist or by pharmacy personnel under the supervision of a pharmacist.
  - ⇨ Including pre-labeled with drug name, strength, dosage form, quantity manufacturer, lot number, beyond-use-date, and the necessary auxiliary labels.
- ✓ The pharmacy maintains a dispensing log, hardcopy prescription, or electronic record that includes the...
  - ⇨ Patient's name and address.
  - ⇨ Drug name, strength, and dosage form.
  - ⇨ Quantity.
  - ⇨ Directions for use.
  - ⇨ Medical practitioner's signature or ID code.
  - ⇨ Medical practitioner's DEA number (for controlled substances only).

ADMINISTRATION OF DRUGS
R4-23-659

PATIENT SELF-ADMINISTRATION OF MEDICATION

Patients CANNOT self-administer drugs in a hospital unless self-administration is ordered by a medical practitioner AND the patient is educated/trained on the proper administration of the drug.

MANAGEMENT OF PATIENT-OWNED DRUGS THAT ENTER THE HOSPITAL
Hospitals must have policies and procedures in place that address what to do when patient-owned drugs are brought into the hospital.
OPTION #1: Allow patient-owned drugs to be administered.
- ✓ The pharmacist or practitioner must first verify the identity of the drug(s) AND the practitioner must write an order specifically for administration of the patient-owned drug.

OPTION #2: Do not allow patient-owned drugs to be administered.
- ✓ The pharmacy must package, seal, and give the drug to an agent of the patient for removal from the hospital OR return the drug to the patient at the time of discharge.

DRUG SAMPLES
The Director of Pharmacy (or the pharmacist-in-charge) is responsible for development, implementation, and compliance with policies and procedures regarding drug samples in the hospital.

INVESTIGATIONAL DRUGS
R4-23-660

ACCESS TO INFORMATION
The Director of Pharmacy or the pharmacist-in-charge must ensure that all available information regarding an investigational drug is available to hospital personnel, such as composition, pharmacology, adverse reactions, administration guidelines, etc.

APPROVAL REQUIRED
The appropriate medical staff committee in a given institution must approve an investigational drug before it can be dispensed.

ROLE OF THE PHARMACY
Investigational drugs must be stored, labeled, and dispensed from the pharmacy.

STERILE COMPOUNDING
R4-23-670

MINIMUM SPACE REQUIREMENT
The sterile compounding area must include at least 100 square feet of contiguous floor. *
* If the permit was issued (or the pharmacy was remodeled) before 11/1/2006, then the minimum area is 60 square feet.

The sterile compounding area must have the following characteristics:
- ✓ Dedicated to preparing and compounding sterile drug products.
- ✓ Isolated from other pharmacy functions.
- ✓ Restricted access.
- ✓ Free from air flow disturbances.
- ✓ Non-porous and cleanable floor, wall, and ceiling.
- ✓ ISO class 7 environment.
    - ⇨ Not required if all compounding occurs inside an ISO class 5 isolator.

EQUIPMENT REQUIREMENTS
The following equipment is required for sterile compounding:
- ✓ Devices that maintain an ISO class 5 environment (e.g. laminar airflow hoods, biological safety cabinets, barrier isolators).
- ✓ Waste containers for needles, syringes, and other sterile compounding waste.
    - ⇨ Also, if applicable, waste containers for chemotherapeutic, cytotoxic, and infectious waste.
- ✓ Freezers (if necessary) with temperature controls and a thermometer.
- ✓ Containers to maintain required drug storage conditions during delivery.
- ✓ Infusion devices and accessories (e.g. infusion pumps and administration sets).
- ✓ Current reference for compounding sterile drug products. This is in addition to the professional reference library requirement outlined in R4-23-612 (see page 69).

POLICIES AND PROCEDURES
Policies and procedures for sterile compounding/dispensing must be established prior to performing compounding activities. These policies and procedures should cover virtually everything, including...
- ✓ Verification of quality and safety.
- ✓ Clinical service and drug monitoring.
- ✓ Controlled substances.
- ✓ Cytotoxic drug handling, storage and disposal.
- ✓ Guidelines for drug administration.
- ✓ Product procurement.
- ✓ Sterile product storage, compounding, and dispensing.
- ✓ Product and process validation testing.
- ✓ Managing drug recalls and expired products.
- ✓ Managing adverse drug reactions.
- ✓ Beyond-use-date determination.
- ✓ Temperature/environmental controls.
- ✓ Sterile product delivery requirements.

As with all other pharmacy policies and procedures, these policies and procedures must be...
- ✓ Assembled into a manual (written or electronic).
- ✓ Made available for employee reference and Board inspection.
- ✓ Reviewed and, if necessary, changed/updated biennially (once every two (2) years).

CERTIFICATION REQUIREMENTS
Cleanrooms (ISO class 7 environments) and laminar air flow hoods (and/or other ISO class 5 equipment) MUST BE CERTIFIED EVERY SIX (6) MONTHS.

STERILE DRUG PRODUCT COMPOUNDING
RISK CATEGORIES
R4-23-670

STANDARD-RISK

Standard-risk sterile products are sterile parenteral or injectable products compounded from sterile commercial drugs using sterile commercial devices, or sterile otic or ophthalmic products compounded using non-sterile ingredients.

THREE (3) AREAS OF CONCERN:
ENVIRONMENT, PROCEDURE, AND ATTIRE.

#1 ENVIRONMENT
✓ Product is compounded in an ISO class 5 environment located within an ISO class 7 environment.

#2 PROCEDURE
✓ Procedures involve only a few closed-system, basic, simple aseptic manipulations.
✓ Compounding personnel must complete an annual media fill test to validate aseptic technique.

#3 ATTIRE
✓ Compounding personnel must wear personal protective equipment (PPE), including a gown, gloves, head cover, and booties. PPE is not required when an ISO class 5 isolator is used outside of an ISO class 7 environment.

SUBSTANTIAL-RISK

Substantial-risk sterile drug products are sterile parenteral or injectable products compounded from non-sterile ingredients.

THREE (3) AREAS OF CONCERN:
ENVIRONMENT, PROCEDURE, AND ATTIRE.

#1 ENVIRONMENT
✓ Product is compounded in an ISO class 5 environment located within an ISO class 7 environment.

#2 PROCEDURE
✓ Compounding personnel must complete an annual media fill test that simulates the most challenging/stressful conditions using dry, non-sterile media to validate aseptic technique.

#3 ATTIRE
✓ Compounding personnel must wear personal protective equipment (PPE), including a gown, gloves, head cover, and booties. PPE is not required when an ISO class 5 isolator is used outside of an ISO class 7 environment.

LIMITED-SERVICE PHARMACIES
R4-23-671

Limited-service pharmacies only practice a "limited segment" of pharmacy.

TYPES OF LIMITED-SERVICE PHARMACIES
- ✓ Correctional pharmacies.
- ✓ Mail-order pharmacies.
- ✓ Long-term care pharmacies.
- ✓ Sterile pharmaceutical products pharmacies.
- ✓ Nuclear pharmacies.

RULES THAT APPLY TO ALL LIMITED-SERVICE PHARMACIES

- ✓ Generally, no one can be inside a limited-service pharmacy unless an authorized pharmacist is present.

- ✓ Everyone in a limited-service pharmacy must wear an ID badge with name and title when on duty.

- ✓ Limited-service pharmacies must comply with the same minimum space requirements as required for other types of pharmacies unless they obtain permission for the Board to operate in smaller spaces. *

    * To obtain approval, the smaller space must enhance pharmacy practice AND benefit the public.

BOARDS OF PHARMACY GENERALLY ARE NOT CONCERNED WITH DE-REGULATING TO THE BENEFIT OF PHARMACIES. THEIR PRIORITY IS TO PROTECT THE PUBLIC.

- ✓ If the Board determines that crowding interferes with safe pharmacy practice, minimum space requirements may be increased.

- ✓ As with all other pharmacies, limited-service pharmacies must establish policies and procedures prior to commencing operation.

LIMITED-SERVICE CORRECTIONAL PHARMACIES
R4-23-672

Limited-service correctional pharmacies are pharmacies located within a correctional facility.

Must adhere to the same standards as other pharmacies (e.g. there must be a pharmacist-in-charge).

MINIMUM SPACE REQUIREMENT
The same floor space and counter space requirements as for retail pharmacy…
- ✓ Floor must be at least 300 square feet + 60 square feet per person working at one time > 3 people.
- ✓ Counter space must be at least 3 square feet/licensee working at one time.
- ✓ Must have a separate patient counseling area.

BARRIER REQUIREMENT
- ✓ When closed, the pharmacy area must be enclosed by permanent floor or counter to ceiling or roof barrier/partition and locked doors.
- ✓ Barrier to prevent unauthorized access during open hours of operation must be at least 66 inches high.

SECURITY REQUIREMENT
- ✓ All areas of a limited-service pharmacy must be locked by key or programmable code.

FACILITY AND EQUIPMENT REQUIREMENTS
Facility requirements that follow R4-23-611 (e.g. clean, sink, toilet, etc.).
Equipment as outlined in R4-23-612 (e.g. graduates, balance, mortar and pestle, reference library, etc.).

ABSENCE OF PHARMACIST
When no pharmacist is on duty in a correctional pharmacy, authorized personnel must have access to remote drug storage areas (essentially the same requirement as for hospital pharmacies).

Remote drug storage areas must…
- ✓ Contain properly labeled drugs that may be needed and administered safely without the pharmacist.
- ✓ Be accessible only with a physician's written order.
- ✓ Provide a written record of each drug removed.
- ✓ Be inventoried at least once weekly.

If a drug is needed to meet the immediate need of a patient and it is not available in the remote drug storage area, there must be procedures for an authorized supervisory nurse to enter the pharmacy to remove the drug.

This nurse must receive training on proper…
- ✓ Pharmacy access.
- ✓ Drug removal.
- ✓ Recordkeeping.

The authorized nurse may only delegate authority to access the pharmacy to another nurse in an emergency.

Information that must be recorded by a nurse when removing a drug from the pharmacy:
- ✓ Patient's name.
- ✓ Drug name, strength, and dosage form.
- ✓ Quantity removed.
- ✓ Date and time of removal.
- ✓ Nurse's signature or initials.

Note: The medication order (or a copy of the medication order) must be attached to this record.

The nurse must place the documentation (described above) in a conspicuous place in the pharmacy.

The pharmacist must verify the drug removal records) within four (4) hours of returning from an absence.

A limited-service correctional pharmacy cannot remain without a pharmacist on duty for more than 96 consecutive hours.

Telephone access to a pharmacist must be arranged before there is no pharmacist on duty.

When a pharmacist is within the correctional facility but absent from the pharmacy and pharmacy technicians remain in the pharmacy to perform their duties, the following apply:
- ✓ All controlled substances must be locked away.
- ✓ All work performed by technicians must be verified by the pharmacist immediately upon his/her return.
- ✓ Drugs that have not been verified by the pharmacist cannot be dispensed/distributed while the pharmacist is absent.

POLICIES AND PROCEDURES

Labels for drugs administered within the facility should follow same rules as hospitals (R4-23-658; see page 78).

Patient self-administration of drugs is generally prohibited (follow R4-23-659; see page 79).

Drugs brought with the patient into the facility must be processed according to procedures (R4-23-659; see page 79).

The Director of Pharmacy is responsible for drug samples (R4-23-659; see page 79).

Use of investigational drugs should follow the same rules as hospitals (R4-23-660; see page 80).

Policies and procedures for a limited-service correctional pharmacy must address virtually every legal/regulatory requirement and every activity in which the pharmacy is or may be involved, such as prescription orders, authorized medical term abbreviations, formulary, clinical services, drug product selection, drug utilization reviews, inventory audits, patient outcome monitoring, etc.

LIMITED-SERVICE MAIL-ORDER PHARMACIES
R4-23-673

MINIMUM SPACE REQUIREMENT $^{R4-23-609}$
Space requirements reflect those of community pharmacies:
- ✓ Floor must be at least 300 square feet + 60 square feet per person working at the same time > 3 people.
- ✓ Counter space must be at least 3 square feet/licensee working at one time.
- ✓ Must have a separate patient counseling area.

Note: Mail-order pharmacies must also provide 30 square feet for each person working in non-dispensing areas. The Board may increase minimum space requirements if crowding interferes with the safe practice of pharmacy.

BARRIER REQUIREMENT
- ✓ When closed, the pharmacy area must be enclosed by permanent floor or counter to ceiling or roof barrier/partition and locked doors.
- ✓ Barrier to prevent unauthorized access during open hours of operation must be at least 66 inches high.

CONTROLLED SUBSTANCE STORAGE REQUIREMENTS
Controlled substances may be either locked in a cabinet/safe or dispersed throughout Rx-only drug stock in a manner that deters theft/diversion.

PRESCRIPTION DELIVERY REQUIREMENT
In compliance with R4-23-402, when a prescription is delivered to the patient and the pharmacist is not present, the following written or printed medication information must accompany the prescription:
- ✓ Approved uses.
- ✓ Potential side effects.
- ✓ Potential drug interactions.
- ✓ Action to take in the event of a missed dose.
- ✓ The phone number of the dispensing pharmacy to consult with a pharmacist. *

---

* LIMITED-SERVICE MAIL-ORDER PHARMACY PHONE NUMBER

- ✓ Phone number must be TOLL-FREE and printed on the label affixed to each dispensed container.
  - ✓ Pharmacist must be available by phone at least five (5) days/week and 40 hours/week.

POLICIES AND PROCEDURES
As with all pharmacies, policies and procedures for limited-service mail-order pharmacies must address virtually every legal/regulatory requirement and every activity in which the pharmacy is or may be involved.

LIMITED-SERVICE LONG-TERM CARE PHARMACY
R4-23-674

PROVIDER PHARMACY REQUIREMENTS
If a limited-service long-term care pharmacy contracts with a long-term care facility to act as a "provider pharmacy" then the pharmacy must additionally comply with R4-23-701, 701.01, 701.02, 701.03, and 701.04 (see pages 91 – 95).

PERMIT AND DISTRIBUTION REQUIREMENTS
Permit and drug distribution standards for limited-service long-term care pharmacies follow R4-23-606 to R4-23-612, which are essentially the same standards as those that apply to community pharmacies.

FORMULARY DEVELOPMENT
Development of a medication formulary is optional and requires collaboration between…
- ✓ The Medical Director.
- ✓ The Director of Nursing.
- ✓ The long-term care consultant pharmacist.
- ✓ The long-term care facility's provider pharmacy.

POLICIES AND PROCEDURES
As with other pharmacies, policies and procedures for limited-service long-term care pharmacies must address virtually every legal/regulatory requirement and every activity in which the pharmacy is or may be involved.

LIMITED-SERVICE STERILE PHARMACEUTICAL PRODUCTS PHARMACIES
R4-23-675

PRESCRIPTION DELIVERY REQUIREMENT
In compliance with R4-23-402, when a prescription is delivered to the patient and the pharmacist is not present, the following written or printed medication information must accompany the prescription:
- ✓ Approved uses.
- ✓ Potential side effects.
- ✓ Potential drug interactions.
- ✓ Action to take in the event of a missed dose.
- ✓ The phone number of the dispensing pharmacy to consult with a pharmacist. *

---

* LIMITED-SERVICE STERILE PHARMACEUTICAL PRODUCTS PHARMACY PHONE NUMBER

- ✓ Phone number must be TOLL-FREE and printed on the label affixed to each dispensed container.
  - ✓ Pharmacist must be available by phone at least five (5) days/week and 40 hours/week.

OTHER REQUIREMENTS
Limited-service sterile pharmaceutical products pharmacies must also comply with R4-23-608 through 612, R4-23-670, and R4-23-671. These regulations pertain to various aspects including minimum space, security, equipment, etc. To review a summary of these regulations, see pages 14, 19, 67 – 69, and 81 – 83.

LIMITED-SERVICE NUCLEAR PHARMACIES
R4-23-681 & R4-23-682

AUTHORIZED NUCLEAR PHARMACIST ELIGIBILITY REQUIREMENTS
- ✓ Current pharmacist license AND
- ✓ Board of Pharmaceutical Specialties (BPS) certification as a nuclear pharmacist OR all of the following:
    - ⇨ Complete 200 hours of didactic training and meet the minimum training requirements for status as an authorized user of radioactive material as specified by the Arizona Radiation Regulatory Agency and the United States Nuclear Regulatory Commission.
    - ⇨ Complete 500 hours of clinical training under supervision of an authorized nuclear pharmacist.
    - ⇨ Certify in writing that the above training was completed (must be signed by the preceptor).

REGULATORY COMPLIANCE
In addition to state and federal pharmacy law, limited-service nuclear pharmacies must also comply with the Arizona Radiation Regulatory Agency and the United States Nuclear Regulatory Commission.

DISTRIBUTION OF RADIOPHARMACEUTICALS
Radiopharmaceuticals must only be transferred to other persons/entities that hold a current Radioactive Materials License issued by the Arizona Radiation Regulatory Agency.

PERMIT REQUIREMENTS
To obtain a permit to operate a limited-service nuclear pharmacy, the applicant must be or employ an authorized nuclear pharmacist with a current Arizona Radiation Regulatory Agency Materials License.

The designated pharmacist-in-charge must be an authorized nuclear pharmacist. This person is responsible for operating the pharmacy, communicating Board directives to other personnel, and complying with state and federal laws and rules.

SUPERVISION REQUIREMENT
An authorized nuclear pharmacist must...
- ✓ Be present when the pharmacy is open for business.
- ✓ Supervise all personnel performing tasks to prepare and distribute radiopharmaceuticals and ancillary products.

MINIMUM SPACE AND FACILITY REQUIREMENTS
Limited-service nuclear pharmacies must have at least...
- ✓ 300 square feet for a radiopharmaceutical compounding and dispensing area that is completely separate from pharmacy areas for non-radioactive drugs. *
- ✓ 80 square feet for a hot lab and storage area.
- ✓ 30 square feet for each person working in non-dispensing areas.

* Non-radioactive drug pharmacy area must comply with space requirements for community pharmacies (i.e. 300 square feet + 60 square feet for each person exceeding three (3) people working at one time).

There must be four (4) separate areas for...
1) Preparing and dispensing radiopharmaceuticals.
2) Receiving and shipping radiopharmaceuticals.
3) Storing radiopharmaceuticals.
4) Decaying radioactive waste.

BARRIER REQUIREMENT
- ✓ When closed, the pharmacy area must be enclosed by permanent floor or counter to ceiling or roof barrier/partition and locked doors.
- ✓ Barrier to prevent unauthorized access during open hours of operation must be at least 66 inches high.

PRESCRIPTION ORDER REQUIREMENTS
In addition to information required to appear on a standard prescription order, radiopharmaceutical prescription orders must also contain the following:
- ✓ Date and time the radiopharmaceutical was calibrated.
- ✓ Name of the procedure for which the radiopharmaceutical is prescribed.
- ✓ The words "Physician's Use Only" rather than the patient's name if the product is a non-therapeutic or non-blood product.

PRESCRIPTION CONTAINER LABEL REQUIREMENTS
In addition to information required to appear on a standard prescription label, the label on the lead container used to store and transport a radiopharmaceutical must also include:
- ✓ Date and time the radiopharmaceutical was calibrated.
- ✓ Name of the procedure for which the radiopharmaceutical is prescribed.
- ✓ The words "Physician's Use Only" rather than the patient's name if the product is a non-therapeutic or non-blood product.
- ✓ Name of the radiopharmaceutical.
- ✓ Molybdenum 99 content to USP limits.
- ✓ The standard radiation symbol.

The immediate container for the radiopharmaceutical (i.e. the container within the lead container) must have a label with this information:
- ✓ The words "Physician's Use Only" for non-therapeutic or non-blood products.
- ✓ Patient's name for therapeutic or blood products.
- ✓ Date and time the radiopharmaceutical was calibrated.
- ✓ Name of the radiopharmaceutical.
- ✓ Dose.
- ✓ Serial number ("Rx number")
- ✓ The words "CAUTION: RADIOACTIVE MATERIAL" & the standard radiation symbol

EQUIPMENT REQUIREMENTS
- ✓ ARRA-approved fume hood. *
- ✓ LAFH.
- ✓ Dose calibrator.
- ✓ Refrigerator.
- ✓ Class A prescription balance or electronic balance of equal or greater accuracy.
- ✓ Well scintillation counter.
- ✓ Incubator oven.
- ✓ Microscope.
- ✓ Various labels.
- ✓ Glassware required by the ARRA. *
- ✓ Other equipment and supplies required by the ARRA. *
- ✓ Current antidote and drug information.
- ✓ Poison control phone number displayed in the pharmacy area.

* Arizona Radiation Regulatory Agency (ARRA)

REFERENCE LIBRARY REQUIREMENT
Must have a current professional reference library consisting of at least one reference or text that addresses therapeutics, nuclear pharmacy practice, and imaging.

Must also have current versions/supplements of the following:
- ✓ ARS § 30-651 through 696 pertaining to the ARRA. *
- ✓ ARRA Rules. *
- ✓ FDA regulations pertaining to radioactive drugs.
- ✓ Arizona Pharmacy Practice Act and Rules.
- ✓ Arizona Uniform Controlled Substances Act.
- ✓ Radiological Health Handbook.

* Arizona Radiation Regulatory Agency (ARRA)

POLICIES AND PROCEDURES
As with other types of pharmacies, policies and procedures for a limited-service nuclear pharmacy must address virtually every legal/regulatory requirement and every activity in which the pharmacy is or may be involved.

PHARMACY LAW
SIMPLIFIED

LONG-TERM CARE CONSULTANT PHARMACISTS
R4-23-701

CONSULTANT PHARMACIST REQUIREMENTS AND RESPONSIBILITIES
- ✓ Current Arizona pharmacist licensure.
- ✓ Provide pharmaceutical care services (defined in R4-23-110 – summarized below).
    - ⇨ Drug selection.
    - ⇨ Drug utilization reviews.
    - ⇨ Drug administration.
    - ⇨ Drug therapy monitoring.
    - ⇨ Otherwise identify and resolve or prevent potential and actual drug-related problems.
- ✓ Review and assist facility in developing policies and procedures for drug/device storage and distribution.
- ✓ Using CMS- and HHS-established* indicators, provide evaluation programs to monitor therapeutic response and utilization of all drugs/devices prescribed to residents.
- ✓ Provide pharmacy education services within the facility.
- ✓ Participate in quality management of resident care in the facility.
- ✓ Communicate with the provider pharmacy to resolve problems and concerns.

*CMS = Centers for Medicare & Medicaid Services; HHS = Department of Health & Human Services.

EMERGENCY DRUG SUPPLY UNITS
The consultant pharmacist must work with medical staff, the director of nursing and the pharmacist-in-charge of the provider pharmacy to provide an emergency drug supply unit within the facility so licensed nursing staff can have access to emergency medications when the provider pharmacy is closed.

LABELS AND PACKAGING
Labels and packaging for all products to be used within the facility must comply with state and federal law.

CONTROLLED SUBSTANCE STORAGE
Unless the facility uses a single-unit package medication distribution system with accurate records of administration/ultimate disposition, then controlled substances must be stored separate from other medications in a locked, permanently affixed compartment.

ACCESS TO INFORMATION
To evaluate the drug use of each resident, the consultant pharmacist must have access to…
- ✓ Patient profiles from the provider pharmacy.
- ✓ Medication administration records from the long-term care facility.
- ✓ Reports of suspected ADRs.
- ✓ Inspection reports of drug storage areas (emphasis on detecting expired drugs).

REPORTING DRUG IRREGULARITIES AND ERRORS
When irregularities and dispensing errors are identified, the consultant pharmacist should notify the prescriber, the director of nursing at the facility, and the provider pharmacy.

DRUGS WITH ILLEGIBLE OR MISSING LABELS

Drugs that have illegible or missing labels must be identified and replaced or re-labeled by the pharmacy that dispensed the medication.

PROVIDER PHARMACIES FOR LONG-TERM CARE FACILITIES
R4-23-701.01

PRESCRIPTION LABEL REQUIREMENTS
When a drug is dispensed by a provider pharmacy for a long-term care resident, the prescription label must comply with ARS § 32-1968, R4-23-701.01, and ARS § 36-2525. These requirements are summarized below.

ARS § 32-1968
- ✓ Pharmacy's name and address.
- ✓ Serial number ("Rx number").
- ✓ Date of dispensing.
- ✓ Prescriber's name.
- ✓ Patient's name.
- ✓ Directions for use.
- ✓ Any cautionary statements contained in the order.

R4-23-701.01
- ✓ Drug name, strength, dosage form, and quantity.
- ✓ Beyond-use-date.

ARS § 36-2525
- ✓ FOR CONTROLLED SUBSTANCES, a statement such as "CAUTION: Federal law prohibits the transfer of this drug to any person other than the patient for whom it was prescribed."

LONG-TERM CARE FACILITY PHARMACY SERVICES EMERGENCY DRUGS
R4-23-701.02

CONTENT AND USE REQUIREMENTS
- ✓ Contents of the emergency drug supply unit must remain the property of the provider pharmacy.
- ✓ The unit must only contain drugs to address immediate emergency medical needs.
- ✓ The unit should only be accessed during emergencies.

LABEL REQUIREMENTS
The individual drugs within an emergency drug supply unit must be labeled with the...
- ✓ Drug name, strength, and dosage form.
- ✓ Manufacturer, lot number, and expiration date.
- ✓ Pharmacy's name address, and phone number.
- ✓ Pharmacist's initials.

The exterior of the emergency drug supply unit must be labeled with...
- ✓ A statement to the effect of "FOR EMERGENCY USE ONLY."
- ✓ A complete list of the contents stored in the unit.
  - ⇨ Drug names, strengths, dosage forms, and quantities.
- ✓ The provider pharmacy's name, address, phone number, and the pharmacist's initials.
- ✓ The expiration date of the drug inside the unit that has the earliest expiration date.
- ✓ The date that the unit was last inspected and the identity of the responsible pharmacist.

TAMPER-EVIDENT SEAL
The unit must also be equipped with a TAMPER-EVIDENT SEAL or something similar.

STORAGE REQUIREMENTS
The emergency drug supply unit must be stored in a temperature-controlled area with a mechanism that prevents access by unauthorized personnel.

LONG-TERM CARE FACILITY PERSONNEL RESPONSIBILITIES
- ✓ Personnel must only remove a drug from the unit after receiving a valid prescription order.
- ✓ Personnel must notify the provider pharmacy when a drug is removed from the unit.

Note: When the unit is automated, the notification described above must be sent electronically.

RECORDKEEPING REQUIREMENTS
If the unit is automated, an electronic record of access must be maintained for at least two (2) years.

POLICIES AND PROCEDURES
Policies and procedures must include at least once weekly exchange or restocking of the unit to ensure an adequate supply of contents exists.

LONG-TERM CARE FACILITY PHARMACY SERVICES EMERGENCY DRUG PRESCRIPTION ORDERS
R4-23-701.03

- ✓ All emergency drug prescription orders must be reviewed by a pharmacist within 72 hours after the first dose is administered.

LONG-TERM CARE FACILITY PHARMACY SERVICES AUTOMATED DISPENSING SYSTEMS
R4-23-701.04

CONTROLLED SUBSTANCE REGISTRATION REQUIREMENTS
The pharmacy permittee or pharmacist-in-charge must obtain a separate controlled substance registration for each location with an automated dispensing system containing controlled substances.

A copy of the registration must be maintained at the provider pharmacy for Board inspection.

DRUG OWNERSHIP
The contents of an automated dispensing system must remain the property of the provider pharmacy.

CONTROLLED SUBSTANCE INVENTORY
When a provider pharmacy performs legally-required controlled substance inventories, controlled substances stored in automated dispensing systems (and emergency drug supply units) must be included in the inventory.
Note: The emergency drug supply unit must be a separate device or container.

SCHEDULE II CONTROLLED SUBSTANCES CANNOT BE STOCKED IN LONG-TERM CARE AUTOMATED DISPENSING SYSTEMS.

REVIEW AND VERIFICATION OF PRESCRIPTION ORDERS
A drug can only be dispensed from an automated dispensing system AFTER a pharmacist reviews and verifies the prescription order.

LABEL REQUIREMENTS
The automated dispensing system must label each drug packet with the same information as required for drugs stored in emergency drug supply units PLUS the resident's room number or the facility identification number.

BARCODE TECHNOLOGY
Automated dispensing systems in long-term care facilities must have barcode (or similar) technology to ensure drugs are loaded accurately.

ELECTRONIC RECORD OF ACCESS
An electronic record of access must be maintained for at least two (2) years; for example, a record of the date and time each user accessed the system and removed a drug.

ELECTRONIC LOG
The provider pharmacy must maintain an electronic log for each container filled by or stocked in an automated dispensing system. The log must include the...
- ✓ Container number.
- ✓ Drug name and strength.
- ✓ NDC number.
- ✓ Manufacturer's lot number and expiration date.
  - ⇨ If container is filled/stocked from multiple stock bottles, list all lot numbers and expiration dates.
- ✓ Date the container was filled.
- ✓ Identity of the licensee that filled the container and the identity of the supervising pharmacist.

The information in the electronic log must be maintained for at least two (2) years for Board inspection.

QUALITY ASSURANCE PROGRAM

There must be an ongoing quality assurance program to monitor system performance and personnel compliance with policies and procedures.

The ongoing quality assurance program must include...
- ✓ Training.
- ✓ Maintenance and calibration.
- ✓ Accuracy validation testing at least once every three (3) months.
- ✓ System downtime and malfunction procedures.

All of these activities must be documented and kept for at least two (2) years for Board inspection.

CONSEQUENCE OF NONCOMPLIANCE

Pharmacies that do not comply with these requirements may be prohibited by the Board from using automated dispensing systems.

HOSPICE INPATIENT FACILITIES
R4-23-702

- ✓ Pharmacies may contract with hospice facilities to provide medications.
- ✓ Prescription drugs can only be dispensed pursuant to a valid prescription.

PRESCRIPTION LABEL REQUIREMENTS
When a drug is dispensed to a hospice inpatient facility patient, the prescription label must comply with ARS § 32-1968, R4-23-702, and ARS § 36-2525. These requirements are summarized below.

ARS § 32-1968
- ✓ Pharmacy's name and address.
- ✓ Serial number ("Rx number").
- ✓ Date of dispensing.
- ✓ Prescriber's name.
- ✓ Patient's name.
- ✓ Directions for use.
- ✓ Any cautionary statements contained in the order.

R4-23-702
- ✓ Drug name, strength, dosage form, and quantity.
- ✓ Beyond-use-date.

ARS § 36-2525
- ✓ FOR CONTROLLED SUBSTANCES, a statement such as "CAUTION: Federal law prohibits the transfer of this drug to any person other than the patient for whom it was prescribed."

DRUGS WITH DAMAGED OR SOILED LABELS

Drugs that have damaged or soiled labels can only be replaced or re-labeled by the pharmacy that dispensed the medication.

EMERGENCY DRUG SUPPLY UNITS
Pharmacies that provide emergency drug supply units to hospice inpatient facilities must follow the same rules as pharmacies that provide these units to long-term care facilities (R4-23-701.02; see pages 92 – 93).

PHARMACIES CANNOT PLACE AUTOMATED DISPENSING SYSTEMS IN HOSPICE INPATIENT FACILITIES.

ASSISTED LIVING FACILITIES
R4-23-703

VALID PRESCRIPTION ORDER REQUIREMENT
Prescription and non-prescription drugs can only be dispensed/sold to an assisted living facility AFTER the pharmacy receives a valid prescription.

PRESCRIPTION LABEL REQUIREMENTS
All drugs dispensed, sold, or delivered to an assisted living facility resident must be labeled in compliance with ARS § 32-1963.01, ARS § 32-1968, ARS § 36-2525, and R4-23-703. These requirements are summarized below.

ARS § 32-1963.01
- If generically substituted, the words: "generic equivalent for [INSERT BRAND NAME]."

ARS § 32-1968
- Pharmacy's name and address.
- Serial number ("Rx number").
- Date of dispensing.
- Prescriber's name.
- Patient's name.
- Directions for use.
- Any cautionary statements contained in the order.

ARS § 36-2525
- FOR CONTROLLED SUBSTANCES, a statement such as "CAUTION: Federal law prohibits the transfer of this drug to any person other than the patient for whom it was prescribed."

R4-23-703
- Drug name, strength, and quantity.
- Beyond-use-date.

DRUGS WITH DAMAGED OR SOILED LABELS

Drugs that have damaged or soiled labels can only be replaced or re-labeled by the pharmacy that dispensed the medication.

EMERGENCY DRUG SUPPLY UNITS
Pharmacies are NOT allowed to provide emergency drug supply units to assisted living facilities.

AUTOMATED DISPENSING SYSTEMS
Pharmacies are NOT allowed to place automated dispensing systems in assisted living facilities.

EMERGENCY DRUG SUPPLY UNITS & AUTOMATED DISPENSING SYSTEMS IN LONG-TERM CARE FACILITIES, HOSPICE INPATIENT FACILITIES, AND ASSISTED LIVING FACILITIES

	LONG-TERM CARE FACILITIES	HOSPICE INPATIENT FACILITIES	ASSISTED LIVING FACILITIES
EMERGENCY DRUG SUPPLY UNITS ALLOWED?	YES	YES	NO
AUTOMATED DISPENSING SYSTEMS ALLOWED?	YES	NO	NO

CUSTOMIZED PATIENT MEDICATION PACKAGES
R4-23-704

With consent from the patient or the patient's caregiver, prescriber, or facility, a pharmacist may dispense medications in customized patient medication packages (e.g. "patient med paks"). When filling prescriptions in this manner, the pharmacist must adhere to USP standards.

DIETARY SUPPLEMENTS
R4-23-801

State law and regulations that apply to drug products also apply to dietary supplements that are labeled or marketed for...
- ✓ Treatment of a disease.
- ✓ Correction of symptom(s) of a disease.
- ✓ Prevention, mitigation, or cure of any disease.

VETERINARY DRUG DISTRIBUTION
R4-23-802

PRESCRIPTION VETERINARY DRUGS

Drug manufacturers or suppliers may distribute prescription veterinary drugs to...
- ✓ Veterinarians.
- ✓ Full-service drug wholesalers.
- ✓ Pharmacies.

NON-PRESCRIPTION VETERINARY DRUGS

Drug manufacturers or suppliers may distribute non-prescription veterinary drugs to...
- ✓ Veterinarians.
- ✓ Full-service drug wholesalers.
- ✓ Pharmacies.
- ✓ Non-prescription drug retailers.

PHARMACY LAW
SIMPLIFIED

RECORDS AND ORDER FORMS
R4-23-1003

If pharmacist-in-charge is replaced, the new pharmacist-in-charge must complete a controlled substance inventory WITHIN 10 DAYS of the change.

CONTROLLED SUBSTANCE INVENTORY RECORD REQUIREMENTS

- ✓ Include an exact count for all Schedule II controlled substances.
- ✓ Include an exact count for all Schedule III, IV, and V controlled substances in containers that hold more than 1,000 dosage units.
- ✓ Include an exact count or estimate for all Schedule III, IV, and V controlled substances in containers that hold equal to or less than 1,000 dosage units.
- ✓ Indicate the date and whether the inventory was taken before opening or after the close of business.
- ✓ Must be signed by the pharmacist-in-charge.
- ✓ Maintain separate from all other records and available for Board inspection for at least three (3) years.

Full-service drug wholesalers and manufacturers must complete an annual controlled substance inventory on May 1st each year. An additional inventory is required in any of the following circumstances:
- ✓ Change in ownership.
- ✓ Discontinuation of business.
- ✓ Within 10 days of a change in the pharmacist-in-charge or designated representative.

CONTROLLED SUBSTANCE LOSS REPORTING REQUIREMENTS

Loss of a controlled substance must be reported to the following three (3) entities on a DEA Form 106 by the pharmacist-in-charge and permittee WITHIN 10 DAYS of discovery:

- ✓ Drug Enforcement Administration (DEA).
- ✓ Narcotic Division of the Department of Public Safety (DPS).
- ✓ Arizona State Board of Pharmacy.

Note: The pharmacy must maintain a copy of the DEA Form 106.

Records that document the manufacturing, re-packaging, or re-labeling of controlled substances must be kept for at least three (3) years.

When controlled substances are received, sold, delivered, or disposed, the records associated with those activities must be kept for at least three (3) years.

FEDERAL PHARMACY LAW HIGHLIGHTS

WHEN FEDERAL LAW AND STATE LAW DIFFER, FOLLOW THE MORE STRINGENT LAW.
When state law and federal law present two different requirements for the same issue, it is important to follow the law that is more restrictive. We commonly observe situations like this with recordkeeping requirements. Generally, federal law requires pharmacies to maintain prescription records for at least two (2) years; whereas, many states require longer prescription record maintenance periods.

THE ROLE OF GOVERNMENT AGENCIES

STATE BOARD OF PHARMACY
- Creates administrative rules to regulate the practice of pharmacy.
  - Includes regulation of traditional compounding pharmacies.
- Enforces state pharmacy laws and rules to protect the health, safety, and welfare of citizens of the state.

FOOD AND DRUG ADMINISTRATION (FDA)
- Enforces drug manufacturing laws.
- Regulates large-scale compounding facilities, also known as "outsourcing facilities."
- Oversees prescription drug advertising, known as "direct-to-consumer" (DTC) advertising.

DRUG ENFORCEMENT ADMINISTRATION (DEA)
- Enforces the federal Controlled Substances Act (CSA).
- Categorizes drugs with potential for abuse, addiction and dependence into controlled substance schedules.

OCCUPATIONAL SAFETY AND HEALTH ADMINISTRATION (OSHA)
- Enforces occupational health and safety laws.

One focus of OSHA is to reduce the risk of employee exposure to blood borne pathogens. This is particularly relevant for locations where employees routinely work with needles, as in pharmacies with a clean room or pharmacies where immunizations are administered.

FEDERAL TRADE COMMISSION (FTC)
- Regulates the advertising of over-the-counter (OTC) drugs, medical devices, cosmetics, and food products.

FEDERAL CONTROLLED SUBSTANCES ACT

The federal Controlled Substances Act (CSA) is located in Title 21 of the Code of Federal Regulations, Part 1300 through 1321 (21 CFR § 1300 – 1321). This section of the study guide highlights and summarizes key points from the CSA. Citations are provided in parenthesis.

✓ The goal of the CSA is to prevent illicit drug use and distribution while allowing for legitimate medical use.

✓ This law is also known as the "Comprehensive Drug Abuse Prevention and Control Act."

✓ The Drug Enforcement Administration (DEA) is responsible for enforcing the CSA.

Note: When reading the original text of the controlled substances act, it is important to recognize that the term "practitioner" is used to describe physicians, dentists, veterinarians, scientific investigators, pharmacies, hospitals, or anyone else permitted to handle controlled substances. (21 CFR § 802)

ACCEPTABLE CONTROLLED SUBSTANCE PRESCRIPTION FORMATS
(21 CFR § 1306.11 & 1306.21)
C-II: Written or Electronic. *
C-III – IV: Written, Verbal, Faxed, or Electronic.
C-V: Written, Verbal, Faxed, Electronic, or OTC. **

* Special cases for Schedule II prescriptions:
   #1 EMERGENCY C-II PRESCRIPTIONS – VERBAL PRESCRIPTION ORDERS PERMITTED
- Schedule II prescription may be dispensed pursuant to verbal order only in an emergency situation.
- Prescription must be communicated directly from the prescriber to the pharmacist.
- Pharmacist must immediately reduce the verbal prescription to writing.
- If prescriber is unknown, pharmacist must make "reasonable effort" to verify validity.
- Quantity must be limited to the amount adequate to treat the patient during the emergency period.
    - The law does not provide specific quantity limits.
- Prescriber must deliver a written hardcopy prescription to the dispensing pharmacy within 7 days.
- The hardcopy prescription should be attached to and kept on file with the verbal order.

   #2 FAXED C-II PRESCRIPTIONS
- Faxed prescription may serve as the "original prescription" for these three (3) patient populations:
   1) Hospice patients.
   2) Home infusion patients.
   3) Long-term care facility residents.
- For all other patient populations, faxed C-II prescriptions may be filled, but cannot be dispensed until the patient presents the original prescription. The pharmacist must verify the original prescription against the faxed prescription prior to dispensing. The pharmacy must keep the original prescription for recordkeeping purposes.

** Limited quantities of a controlled substance may be dispensed without a prescription if state law permits.

ELECTRONIC CONTROLLED SUBSTANCE PRESCRIPTIONS (21 CFR § 1306.08)
Federal law permits e-prescribing of C-II through C-V controlled substances as long as the prescriber and pharmacy use e-prescription software that meets DEA requirements.

CONTROLLED SUBSTANCE PRESCRIPTION REFILLS
C-II: Refills NOT permitted. (21 CFR § 1306.12)
C-III – IV: Up to 5 refills. (21 CFR § 1306.22)
C-V: No maximum.

CONTROLLED SUBSTANCE PRESCRIPTION EXPIRATION
C-II: No expiration.
C-III – IV: Expires 6 months after date written. (21 CFR § 1306.22)
C-V: No expiration.

CONTROLLED SUBSTANCE PRESCRIPTION PARTIAL FILLS
C-II: One partial fill is permitted as long as the remainder can be filled within 72 hours. If the partial fill is not completed within 72 hours, the remainder is void and the prescriber must be notified. * (21 CFR § 1306.13)

C-III – V: Permitted with no time limit for completion; however, keep in mind that C-III and C-IV prescriptions expire 6 months after the date written.

* EXCEPTION: For long-term care or terminally ill patients, multiple partial fills for Schedule II prescriptions are permitted for up to 60 days from the date written. (21 CFR § 1306.13)

SEMANTICS OF THE 5 REFILL LIMIT FOR C-III AND C-IV PRESCRIPTIONS
Mary has a prescription for 30 tablets of Ativan® with instructions to take one (1) tablet by mouth nightly as needed with 5 REFILLS. Imagine that Mary requests just 15 tablets each time she has the prescription filled.

IN SCENARIOS LIKE THE ONE DESCRIBED ABOVE, A PHARMACIST MAY CONSIDER THE FOLLOWING...
Schedule III & IV controlled substance prescriptions are limited to 5 refills within 6 months from the date issued. If Mary receives 15 tablets per fill, must she forfeit the prescribed quantity that remains after the 5th fill?

The answer is NO. In this case, the first 15 tablets are considered to be a "partial fill." The next 15 tablets would represent a completion of the partial fill. This cycle would continue until the patients receives all 180 tablets prescribed, or until the prescription expires, whichever comes first.

MAIN POINT: The number of times a C-III or C-IV prescription is filled is not important. What is important?

#1 THE PRESCRIBER CANNOT AUTHORIZE MORE THAN 5 REFILLS.
#2 THE PATIENT CANNOT RECEIVE A QUANTITY ABOVE THAT WHICH IS PRESCRIBED.

TRANSFERRING CONTROLLED SUBSTANCE PRESCRIPTION ORDERS FOR REFILL
C-II: Transfers are NOT permitted.
C-III – V: May be transferred to another pharmacy on a one-time basis between two licensed pharmacists. *
  * Transfers are unlimited for pharmacies that share a real-time, online database. (21 CFR § 1306.25)

MAINTENANCE OF CONTROLLED SUBSTANCE PRESCRIPTION RECORDS
C-II: Must be stored separate from all other prescription records. (21 CFR § 1304.04)
C-III – V: Must be stored either separate from all other prescription records, or marked in the lower right corner with the letter "C" at least 1-inch high in red ink and stored in the same file with non-controlled substance prescription records. (21 CFR § 1304.04)

CONTROLLED SUBSTANCE STORAGE & SECURITY
Controlled substances must be stored in a locked cabinet or dispersed among non-controlled stock in such a manner as to deter theft or diversion. (21 CFR § 1301.75)

DISTRIBUTING OR RECEIVING CONTROLLED SUBSTANCE INVENTORY
C-II: Use a DEA Form 222 to document the transaction. * (21 CFR § 1305.03)
C-III – V: Use an INVOICE to document the transaction.
  * The Controlled Substance Ordering System (CSOS) is an electronic alternative to the DEA Form 222.

THE "5% RULE" FOR PHARMACIES
Pharmacies that are registered with the DEA may distribute a limited number of controlled substance dosage units to another DEA-registered pharmacy or practitioner WITHOUT REGISTERING AS A DISTRIBUTOR. The limit is 5% of the total number of controlled substance dosage units dispensed during one (1) calendar year.

TO DISPENSE A QUANTITY OF CONTROLLED SUBSTANCE DOSAGE UNITS IN EXCESS OF 5% OF THE TOTAL QUANTITY DISPENSED DURING ONE (1) CALENDAR YEAR, A PHARMACY MUST REGISTER AS A DISTRIBUTOR.

Records of distribution and receipt must be maintained for at least 2 years.
- ✓ Executed DEA Form 222 for C-II drugs.
- ✓ Invoices for C-III, IV, and V drugs.

DISPOSAL OF CONTROLLED SUBSTANCE INVENTORY (21 CFR 1317.05)
Controlled substance inventory that is expired or otherwise unusable should be disposed of promptly by any of these methods:
- ✓ Destroy the substance on-site (i.e. in the pharmacy/facility) in the presence of a DEA agent or other authorized person.
    - o Permission from DEA must be obtained in advance. *
    - o Two (2) employees of the DEA registrant must witness destruction. (21 CFR 1317.95)
    - o No specific method of destruction is required, but the drug must be rendered "non-retrievable."
    - o Document destruction on a DEA Form 41.
- ✓ Deliver the substance to a reverse distributor.
    - o Document transaction on a DEA Form 222.
- ✓ For returns or recalls, deliver the substance to the source from which it was obtained.
    - o Document transaction on a DEA Form 222.
- ✓ Request assistance from the Special Agent in Charge at the local DEA office.
    - o Submit DEA Form 41 to the Special Agent in Charge.
    - o Wait to receive disposal instructions.

* Practitioners (i.e. prescribers, pharmacies, and hospitals) that routinely dispose of controlled substances can obtain special authorization from the DEA to dispose of controlled substances without first obtaining permission. These practitioners must maintain disposal records and report a summary of disposal activities periodically to the DEA Special Agent in Charge.

CONTROLLED SUBSTANCE DRUG WASTAGE
According to a DEA letter to registrants that was written on September 9, 2014, destruction of controlled substance drug wastage in an institutional setting, such as that which is produced when a nurse administers only a fraction of a controlled substance from a pre-filled syringe, should be recorded in compliance with 21 CFR 1304.22(c). A key point here is that the destruction of controlled substance drug wastage in an institutional setting should NOT be recorded on a DEA Form 41.

OTHER KEY POINTS REGARDING CONTROLLED SUBSTANCES

- A controlled substance prescription must be issued for a legitimate medical purpose in the practitioner's usual course of professional practice. (21 CFR § 1306.04)
- The dispensing pharmacist shares a corresponding responsibility with prescriber for proper prescribing and dispensing of controlled substances. (21 CFR § 1306.04)
- Prescriber "post-dating" of prescription issue dates (i.e. writing a "written date" that is later than actual) is prohibited.
- Prescribers are allowed to issue multiple C-II prescriptions to the same patient for the same medication, as long as they indicate the earliest fill date on each prescription AND the total amount prescribed does not exceed a 90-day supply. (21 CFR § 1306.12)
- It is illegal for a patient to mail/ship controlled substances out of the country.
- Federal law places no limit on the number of dosage units of a controlled substance that can be authorized by prescription at one time.
- Verbal orders/prescriptions for controlled substances must be communicated directly FROM THE PRESCRIBER TO THE PHARMACIST. To be clear, pharmacy technicians CANNOT accept oral prescriptions for controlled substances, and agents of the prescriber (e.g. nurses, medical assistants, and secretaries) CANNOT provide telephone authorization for controlled substance prescriptions. (21 CFR 1306.21)
- An agent of the prescriber (e.g. a nurse, medical assistant, or secretary) CAN fax a controlled substance prescription to the pharmacy as long as the prescription is manually signed by the prescriber prior to faxing. (21 CFR 1306.21)

PHARMACY LAW
SIMPLIFIED

REQUIRED INFORMATION FOR CONTROLLED SUBSTANCE PRESCRIPTION ORDERS (21 CFR § 1306.05)

- ✓ Patient's Full Name & Address.
- ✓ Prescriber's Full Name & Address.
- ✓ Prescriber's DEA Number.
- ✓ Drug Name, Strength, & Dosage Form.
- ✓ Quantity Prescribed.
- ✓ Directions for Use.
- ✓ Date Issued.
- ✓ Prescriber's Signature. *

* Not required for verbal prescriptions.

DEA REGISTRATION

- ✓ Required for all practitioners who prescribe controlled substances and all entities involved in the production and/or distribution of controlled substances. Registrants receive a DEA number.
  - ✓ DEA registrations must be renewed once every 3 years.

OVER-THE-COUNTER CONTROLLED SUBSTANCE SALES (21 CFR § 1306.26)

Limited quantities of controlled substances may be dispensed without a prescription if state law permits.

LIMITS
- ✓ 8 ounces (240 mL) of an opium-containing liquid drug product.
- ✓ 4 ounces (120 mL) of a liquid that contains a controlled substance other than opium.
- ✓ 48 dosage units of an opium-containing solid drug product.
- ✓ 24 dosage units of a solid drug product that contains a controlled substance other than opium.

RECORDKEEPING REQUIREMENTS
- ✓ Purchaser must be at least 18 years-old.
- ✓ Purchaser must furnish ID.
- ✓ The pharmacy must record:
  - ○ Name & address of purchaser.
  - ○ Name & quantity of controlled substance sold over-the-counter.
  - ○ Date of sale.
  - ○ Name or initials of dispensing pharmacist.

Per 21 CFR § 1304.04, controlled substance records must be kept for at least 2 years.

CONTROLLED SUBSTANCE INVENTORY REQUIREMENTS (21 CFR § 1304.11)

INITIAL INVENTORY
An initial inventory must be taken when a pharmacy first opens for business.

BIENNIAL INVENTORY
Entire controlled substance inventory must be counted at least once every 2 years.

NEWLY SCHEDULED DRUG OR CHANGE IN SCHEDULE OF A DRUG
When a drug is newly scheduled as a controlled substance or the scheduling of a drug is changed, an inventory is required for the affected drug on the day that the scheduling or change in scheduling takes effect.

INVENTORY COUNTING PROCEDURES

For C-II controlled substances, an EXACT COUNT or measure of every container is required regardless of size.
For C-III, C-IV, and C-V controlled substances...
- ✓ An ESTIMATE or exact count is acceptable for opened containers that hold ≤ 1,000 tablets or capsules.
- ✓ An EXACT COUNT is required for opened containers that hold >1,000 tablets or capsules.

Note: Controlled substance DRUG SAMPLES are not exempt from inventory requirements.
Per 21 CFR § 1304.04, controlled substance records must be kept for at least 2 years.

DRUG ADDICTION TREATMENT ACT OF 2000 (DATA 2000)

- ✓ Allows prescribers to obtain a waiver so they can prescribe Schedule III, IV, and V controlled substances for the treatment of opioid addiction outside of a registered narcotic treatment facility.

- ✓ Does NOT permit the prescribing of Schedule II controlled substances (i.e. methadone) for the treatment of opioid addiction outside of a registered narcotic treatment facility.

- ✓ Prescribers who have obtained the waiver possess a second DEA number that begins with the letter X.

METHADONE DISPENSING RESTRICTIONS

Only registered narcotic treatment facilities can dispense Schedule II controlled substances (i.e. methadone) for the treatment of opioid addiction. These facilities must complete a DEA Form 363 to apply for DEA registration.

DISPENSING METHADONE FROM A PHARMACY

⇨ Dispensing methadone for the treatment of PAIN is PERMITTED.
⇨ Dispensing methadone for the treatment of ADDICTION is PROHIBITED.

PHARMACY LAW
SIMPLIFIED

DEA FORMS

The Drug Enforcement Administration (DEA) is responsible for enforcing the federal Controlled Substances Act (CSA). The DEA's goal is to ensure that controlled substances are available for legitimate medical and research purposes, while preventing illicit use and illegal distribution. To accomplish this, the DEA strictly monitors the manufacturing, distribution, and dispensing of controlled substances. Consequently, extensive documentation is required for legitimate handling of controlled substances. To standardize recordkeeping procedures, the DEA provides preformatted forms for pharmacies and other individuals/entities that handle controlled substances. Use the chart below to memorize the titles of the most commonly used forms ("DEA Form Number") and their associated purposes.

FORM NUMBER	PURPOSE
DEA Form 41	For reporting the destruction of controlled substances.
DEA Form 104	For reporting a pharmacy closure or surrender of a pharmacy permit.
DEA Form 106	For reporting the loss or theft of controlled substances.
DEA Form 222	For ordering Schedule I & II controlled substances.
DEA Form 222a	For ordering an additional supply of DEA 222 forms.
DEA Form 224	For applying for a DEA registration number.
DEA Form 224a	For renewing DEA registration (renewal is required every 3 years).

In pharmacy, the most commonly used DEA form is the DEA Form 222. For that reason, pharmacists should be very familiar with this particular form and its use. See below for an outline of important details:
Each DEA Form 222 includes 2 carbon copies (the original, plus 2 attached copies):
1) The first page (the original) is brown.
    o   Must be retained by the drug supplier.
2) The second page (the first carbon copy) is green.
    o   Must be forwarded to the DEA by the drug supplier.
3) The third page (the second carbon copy) is blue.
    o   Must be retained by the pharmacy.

MISTAKES CANNOT BE CORRECTED

In the event of an error, all copies of the DEA Form 222 must be voided and retained by the pharmacy.

REAL-WORLD SCENARIO

When ordering Schedule II controlled substances for your pharmacy, what must you do with the first two pages (brown and green) of the DEA Form 222?
Give them to the supplier without separating them. For the form to be valid from the supplier's perspective, the brown and green copies must be intact with the carbon paper between them. The pharmacy must retain the third page (blue copy) of the form for recordkeeping purposes.

Note: Pharmacies must keep all controlled substance records (including executed DEA forms) for at least 2 years.

ELECTRONIC ALTERNATIVE TO THE DEA FORM 222

The Controlled Substance Ordering System (CSOS) is an electronic alternative to the DEA Form 222.

PROFESSIONALS WITH PRESCRIBING AUTHORITY

There are two categories of prescribing authority: full authority and limited authority. Four types of healthcare practitioners have full prescribing authority: licensed physicians, dentists, podiatrists, and veterinarians. These practitioners can prescribe any medication within their scope of practice. The "within their scope of practice" part is important. This means veterinarians cannot prescribe medication for humans; dentists cannot prescribe medication for conditions of the eye, etc. Below, we have illustrated the four types of healthcare professionals and the respective academic degrees that confer full prescribing authority. Keep in mind, in addition to meeting the educational requirements, these practitioners must also obtain a license by passing certain board examinations and meeting other regulatory requirements.

PRACTITIONERS WITH <u>FULL</u> PRESCRIBING AUTHORITY

PHYSICIANS
Doctor of Medicine (MD)
Doctor of Osteopathic Medicine (DO)

PODIATRISTS
Doctor of Podiatric Medicine (DPM)

DENTISTS
Doctor of Dental Medicine (DMD)
Doctor of Dental Surgery (DDS)

VETERINARIANS
Doctor of Veterinary Medicine (DVM)

Optometrists and midlevel practitioners have limited prescribing authority. Depending on the state in which they practice, optometrists have certain restrictions and/or limitations regarding what they can prescribe, especially when it comes to controlled substances. The same is true for midlevel practitioners, such as physician assistants and nurse practitioners. Additionally, midlevel practitioners can only prescribe specific medications as outlined in a signed, written agreement with their supervising physician. A licensed physician must approve every prescription written by a midlevel practitioner.

PRACTITIONERS WITH <u>LIMITED</u> PRESCRIBING AUTHORITY

OPTOMETRISTS
Doctor of Optometry (OD)

MIDLEVEL PRACTITIONERS
Physician Assistant (PA)
Nurse Practitioner (NP)

Note: Some states grant limited prescribing authority to additional groups of qualified healthcare professionals, such as certified nurse midwives, certified registered nurse anesthetists, chiropractors, and registered pharmacists.

DEA NUMBER VERIFICATION

Sample DEA#: MH4836726

A prescriber cannot legally issue a controlled substance prescription unless he/she possesses a valid DEA registration number. That number must appear on the face of every controlled substance prescription issued by the prescriber. You may want to verify a DEA number before dispensing a controlled substance, especially if forgery is suspected. DEA numbers are composed of 2 letters followed by 7 numbers. First, we will review the letters.

THE 1ST LETTER: Functions to identify the type of practitioner/registrant.
- A, B, or F for physicians, dentists, veterinarians, hospitals, and pharmacies.
- M for midlevel practitioners.
- P or R for manufacturers, distributors, researchers, and narcotic treatment programs.

> **Note:** Practitioners with a waiver to prescribe buprenorphine (e.g. Subutex® and Suboxone®) for the treatment of opioid addiction outside of a narcotic treatment facility have an additional DEA number that begins with the letter X.

THE 2ND LETTER: Matches the first letter of the prescriber's last name or the first letter of the business name.

Once the letters have been verified, proceed to the 4-step process for the verifying the numerical portion of a DEA number, which is outlined below.

THE 4-STEP PROCESS FOR VERIFYING THE NUMERICAL PORTION OF A DEA NUMBER:

---------STEP 1---------
Add the 1st, 3rd, and 5th digits of the DEA number.

---------STEP 2---------
Add the 2nd, 4th, and 6th digits of the DEA number and multiply the sum by 2.

> **Note:** Remember to multiply the correct set of numbers by 2. Many students mistakenly multiply the sum of the 1st, 3rd, and 5th digits by 2 and get the wrong answer.

---------STEP 3---------
Add your answers from STEP 1 and STEP 2.

---------STEP 4---------
The sum obtained in STEP 3 will be a 2-digit number. If the DEA number is legitimate, then the second digit of this 2-digit number will match the 7th and final digit (known as the "check digit") of the DEA number.

⊃ TRY IT YOURSELF! ⊂

Analyze the sample DEA# shown at the top of this page. You should conclude that the number is valid. Once finished, continue to the "practice problem" shown on the following page.

FEDERAL GOVERNMENT PRACTITIONER EXEMPTION [21 CFR § 1301.23]

Practitioners who are officials of the US Army, Navy, Marines, Air Force, Coast Guard, Public Health Service, or Bureau of Prisons are not required to register with the DEA to prescribe controlled substances, unless they work in private practice. In place of the DEA number, these practitioners must indicate their branch of service or the agency in which they serve and their service identification number (e.g. "Army 123-45-6789").

PHARMACY LAW
SIMPLIFIED

DEA NUMBER VERIFICATION
PRACTICE PROBLEM

VERIFY THE DEA NUMBER DISPLAYED BELOW.

John Smith, MD
DEA # FS8524616

SOLUTION

THE 1ST LETTER: The registrant is a physician (MD), so the first letter must be "A, B, or F."
THE 2ND LETTER: The prescriber's last name is Smith, so the second letter must be "S."

---------STEP 1---------

Add the 1st, 3rd, and 5th digits of the DEA number.

⇨ The sum of the 1st, 3rd, and 5th numbers (8 + 2 + 6) is 16.

---------STEP 2---------

Add the 2nd, 4th, and 6th digits of the DEA number and multiply the sum by 2.

⇨ The sum of the 2nd, 4th, and 6th numbers (5 + 4 + 1) is 10, and 10 x 2 = 20.

Note: Remember to multiply the correct set of numbers by 2. Many students mistakenly multiply the sum of the 1st, 3rd, and 5th digits by 2 and get the wrong answer.

---------STEP 3---------

Add your answers from STEP 1 and STEP 2.

⇨ The sum of 16 and 20 is 36.

---------STEP 4---------

Verify that the final digit of your answer from STEP 3 matches the check digit of the DEA number.

⇨ The final digit of the answer from STEP 3 is the number 6, which matches the check digit of the DEA number.

✓

**ACCORDING TO THE ANALYSIS OUTLINED ABOVE,
THIS DEA NUMBER APPEARS TO BE LEGITIMATE.**

Note: The Drug Addiction Treatment Act of 2000 (DATA 2000) requires prescribers to include their special DEA number (which begins with the letter X) on buprenorphine prescriptions issued for the treatment of opioid addiction. For example, Dr. John Smith's special DEA number (if he had one) would look like this: XS8524616.

INSTITUTIONAL DEA NUMBERS

When acting in the usual course of employment, practitioners and residents working for an institution (e.g. hospital) may prescribe controlled substances using the institution's DEA number. Institutions must assign an internal code number to each practitioner. The practitioner must append this code to the end of the institution's DEA number when writing prescriptions for controlled substances. See below for an example.

INSTITUTION'S DEA NUMBER   PRACTITIONER'S INTERNAL CODE
⇩   ⇩

AB8524616 - 1234

Each institution must keep a list of practitioners and their assigned internal codes to enable other DEA registrants, such as pharmacies, to contact the institution and verify that a particular practitioner is authorized to prescribe controlled substances.

COMBAT METHAMPHETAMINE EPIDEMIC ACT OF 2005 (CMEA)

This law imposes regulations on the over-the-counter sale of solid dosage forms (including gel caps) that contain pseudoephedrine, ephedrine, and phenylpropanolamine. These substances are precursors to either amphetamine or methamphetamine.

PRECURSOR		POTENTIAL END PRODUCT
Pseudoephedrine	⇨	Methamphetamine
Ephedrine	⇨	Methamphetamine
Phenylpropanolamine	⇨	Amphetamine

PRIOR TO PURCHASING, THE CUSTOMER MUST FURNISH PHOTO ID.

OTC PURCHASE LIMITS
- ✓ Daily: 3.6 grams/day
- ✓ Monthly: 9 grams/month

Per 21 CFR § 844(a), a maximum of 7.5 grams of the monthly 9-gram limit can be obtained by mail.

PHARMACY RECORDKEEPING REQUIREMENTS
- ✓ Product name & quantity sold.
- ✓ Name, address, & signature of purchaser.
- ✓ Date & time of sale.

Records must be maintained for at least 2 years.

LIMITS DO NOT APPLY WHEN OBTAINED BY PRESCRIPTION.

PHARMACY STORAGE REQUIREMENT
Solid dosage forms (including gel caps) that contain pseudoephedrine, ephedrine, or phenylpropanolamine must be be stored behind the pharmacy counter or in a locked cabinet away from customers.

MANUFACTURER PACKAGING REQUIREMENT
Solid dosage forms (including gel caps) that contain pseudoephedrine, ephedrine, or phenylpropanolamine must be packaged in blister packs (see illustration below).

POISON PREVENTION PACKAGING ACT OF 1970 (PPPA)

- ✓ Enacted to reduce the incidence of death and serious injury caused when children access and consume medications and other dangerous household substances (e.g. household cleaning agents).

- ✓ Requires most medications to be dispensed in child-resistant packages (e.g. child safety caps on prescriptions dispensed from a pharmacy).

- ✓ Containers must be "significantly difficult" for children under 5 years-old to open, but not difficult for adults.

- ✓ Exceptions to the child-resistant packaging requirement include…
    - Nitroglycerin Sublingual Tablets
    - Steroid Dose Packs
    - Aerosols
    - Birth Control Pills
    - Female Hormone Replacement Drugs

NITROGLYCERIN SUBLINGUAL TABLETS ARE THE MOST NOTEWORTHY EXCEPTION TO THE CHILD-RESISTANT PACKAGING REQUIREMENT.

If an adult has difficulty with or is unable to open a prescription bottle equipped with a child safety cap (e.g. due to arthritis), then the patient may request an easy-open cap (also referred to as a "snap cap"). The prescribing practitioner may also request an easy-open cap on behalf of the patient by making a notation on the face of the prescription.

OMNIBUS BUDGET RECONCILIATION ACT OF 1990 (OBRA '90)

- ✓ Requires pharmacists to perform prospective drug utilization reviews (DURs) and offer counseling to Medicaid patients. When performing a DUR, the pharmacist should look for things like…
    - Therapeutic duplications.
    - Drug-disease contraindications.
    - Drug-drug interactions.
    - Incorrect doses.
    - Inappropriate durations of treatment.
    - Drug-allergy interactions.
    - Clinical abuse/misuse.

- ✓ To contract with Medicaid, pharmacies must implement standards to provide counseling to Medicaid patients. The "offer to counsel" requirement does not apply in inpatient settings.

- ✓ Pharmacists must make a reasonable effort to keep patient profiles up-to-date.

- ✓ This specific law pertains only to Medicaid patients, but states have expanded it to apply to all patients.

HEALTH INSURANCE PORTABILITY & ACCOUNTABILITY ACT (HIPAA)

Protects the privacy and security of patient medical records and health information ("protected health information" or "PHI").

HIPAA PRIVACY RULE
- ✓ Limits the use and disclosure of protected health information (PHI) to the "minimum necessary."
- ✓ Provides an option for the patient to obtain a copy of their health record and request corrections.

HIPAA SECURITY RULE
- ✓ Requires various administrative, physical, and technical safeguards to ensure the confidentiality, integrity, and overall security of protected health information including electronic medical records.
- ✓ Outlines national standards for healthcare providers, insurance companies, and healthcare financial claim processing companies to protect the privacy of individual health information.

HIPAA BREACH NOTIFICATION RULE
- ✓ If protected health information has been exposed to unauthorized individuals, the affected patient(s) must be notified.

WHEN "MINIMUM NECESSARY USE AND DISCLOSURE" DOES NOT APPLY
- Disclosures to a healthcare provider for treatment.
- Disclosures to the patient upon request.
- Disclosures authorized by the patient.
- Disclosures necessary to comply with other laws.
- Disclosures to the Department of Health and Human Services (HHS) for a compliance investigation, review, or enforcement.

PRACTICAL MEASURES FOR PROTECTING PATIENT HEALTH INFORMATION
- Maintain a reasonable distance between the patient with whom you are speaking and other people in the area to prevent sensitive information from being overheard.
- Speak loudly enough for the patient to hear you, but not loud enough for bystanders to hear.
- Do not shout to a patient when discussing PHI such as medication names, medical conditions, date of birth, address, and other sensitive information.
- Never gossip about a patient and their medical information.
- Do not disclose PHI to anyone over the phone who is not legitimately entitled the information.

**PHARMACY LAW
SIMPLIFIED**

GENERIC SUBSTITUTION AND THE ORANGE BOOK

Prescribers often issue prescriptions for brand name drug products, but we help patients save a lot of money by dispensing generic equivalents. Another term for "generic equivalent" is "therapeutic equivalent." Compared to a brand product, the generic or therapeutic equivalent is equal in terms of strength, quality, performance, safety, intended use, dosage form, route of administration, and rate and extent of absorption... pretty much every category that matters from a medical and scientific standpoint. The only difference between a brand product and a generic equivalent is the identity of the manufacturer and the composition of inactive ingredients (e.g. fillers, binders, and color additives).

THE FEDERAL ORANGE BOOK

- ✓ OFFICIAL TITLE: Approved Drug Products with Therapeutic Equivalence Evaluations

DETERMINATION OF THERAPEUTIC EQUIVALENCE

The Federal Orange Book contains a listing of "TE codes" (therapeutic equivalence codes) for generic drug products. Products with a TE code beginning with the letter A are deemed to be therapeutically equivalent to the brand name product. Pharmacists commonly refer to these products as "A-rated generics."

REAL-WORLD SCENARIO

You receive a prescription for Lipitor® over the telephone. Should you dispense brand name Lipitor® or the generic equivalent, atorvastatin?
Atorvastatin. If the prescriber (or his/her agent) expressly stated that the brand name is necessary and substitution is not permitted, then it would have been appropriate to dispense the brand name version instead.

NARROW THERAPEUTIC INDEX DRUGS

A narrow therapeutic index (NTI) drug is a medication that requires careful dose titration and patient monitoring for safe & effective use. For a drug to be considered "NTI," one of the following two conditions must apply:
- There is less than a 2-fold difference between the median lethal dose (LD50) and the median effective dose (ED50).
- There is less than a 2-fold difference between the minimum toxic concentration (MTC) and the minimum effective concentration (MEC).

Note: ED50 is the dose that produces the desired effect in 50% of the population, and LD50 is the dose that is lethal in 50% of the population.

TRUE OR FALSE

A BRAND NAME NARROW THERAPEUTIC INDEX DRUG SHOULD NOT BE SUBSTITUTED WITH A GENERIC DRUG.
It depends. The pharmacist must use professional judgement combined with regulatory knowledge to make the final determination in any generic substitution decision.

FEDERAL FOOD, DRUG & COSMETIC ACT (FD&C ACT)

The first federal law to regulate drug products was the Pure Food and Drug Act of 1906. This legislation addressed purity, but did not address safety or prohibit false claims. In 1938, the Pure Food and Drug Act was replaced by the Food, Drug, and Cosmetic Act (FD&C Act). This new legislation required drug manufacturers to provide the FDA with evidence of safety by submitting a New Drug Application (NDA); however, if action was not taken by the FDA within 60 days, the drug was automatically approved. The FD&C Act has undergone several amendments since it was first passed in 1938. In this section of the study guide, we highlight key amendments and their impact on the practice of pharmacy.

DURHAM-HUMPHREY AMENDMENT (1951)
- ✓ Drug products are separated into two categories: over-the-counter and prescription-only ("legend drugs").
- ✓ Legend drug labels must state, "Caution: Federal law prohibits dispensing without a prescription."

KEFAUVER HARRIS AMENDMENT (1962)
- ✓ Passed in reaction to "The Thalidomide Tragedy," which took place between 1957 – 1961.
- ✓ To obtain FDA approval for a drug, manufacturers must provide substantial evidence of safety and efficacy.
- ✓ Previously, New Drug Applications gained automatic approval after 60 days if the FDA did not take action. With this amendment, manufacturers must prove safety regardless of the timeframe.
- ✓ In the past, manufacturers were not required to prove efficacy.

FEDERAL ANTI-TAMPERING ACT (1982)
- ✓ Passed in reaction to the "Chicago Tylenol® Murders," which took place in 1982.
- ✓ Over-the-counter (OTC) drug products must have a tamper-evident seal.

PRESCRIPTION DRUG MARKETING ACT OF 1987 (PDMA)
- ✓ Banned the selling/purchasing/trading of prescription drug samples.

The Dietary Supplement Health and Education Act of 1994 (DSHEA)
- ✓ Dietary supplements (e.g. vitamins, minerals, herbal supplements) are classified as "food" since they supplement the diet. As a result, manufacturers can market dietary supplements without FDA review.
- ✓ For drug products, a manufacturer must prove safety before entering the market, but for food products the FDA must prove lack of safety to be able to take a product off the market.

FOOD AND DRUG ADMINISTRATION MODERNIZATION ACT OF 1997 (FDAMA)
- ✓ The statement required to appear on legend drug labels per the Durham-Humphrey Amendment ("Caution: Federal law prohibits dispensing without a prescription") could be shortened to "Rx only."

ADULTERATED VS MISBRANDED

ADULTERATED	MISBRANDED
Problem(s) with the PRODUCT, such as the…	Problem(s) with the LABELING, such as…
✓ Strength of the product.	✓ False information.
✓ Quality of the product.	✓ Misleading information.
✓ Purity of the product.	✓ Insufficient information.

COMPOUNDING VS MANUFACTURING

When pharmacies cross the line into manufacturing, they expose themselves to many legal/regulatory liabilities. For instance, manufacturers must obtain a drug manufacturer permit and register with the FDA prior to commencing operation. Manufacturers are also required to comply with current good manufacturing practices (CGMP). Compounding pharmacies do not share these burdens.

THE DEFINITION OF COMPOUNDING

COMPOUNDING IS THE CREATION OF PERSONALIZED, PATIENT-SPECIFIC MEDICATIONS.

- A compounded drug product CANNOT BE A COPY of a commercially available FDA-approved product. *
- A compounded drug product cannot contain any ingredient that has been deemed unsafe or ineffective.
- A product can ONLY be compounded AFTER RECEIVING AN INDIVIDUAL, PATIENT-SPECIFIC PRESCRIPTION ORDER OR IN ANTICIPATION OF RECEIVING A PATIENT-SPECIFIC PRESCRIPTION ORDER IF AN ESTABLISHED PRESCRIBING PATTERN EXISTS.

* Possible exception in the event of a shortage.

Compounding must take place in a registered pharmacy under the supervision of a licensed pharmacist. Manufacturing must take place in a registered drug manufacturing facility.

OUTSOURCING FACILITIES

Per the Drug Quality and Security Act of 2013, large-scale compounding facilities, also referred to as "outsourcing facilities," must register with the FDA as outsourcing facilities and comply with current good manufacturing practices (CGMP).

REGULATED BY...	TRADITIONAL PHARMACIES	OUTSOURCING FACILITIES	MANUFACTURING FACILITIES
STATE BOARD OF PHARMACY	✓	✓	✓
FOOD AND DRUG ADMINISTRATION		✓	✓

MEDICAID TAMPER-RESISTANT PRESCRIPTION REQUIREMENT

Written outpatient prescriptions billed to Medicaid must be written on tamper-resistant paper to reduce the incidence of Medicaid insurance fraud. The tamper-resistant prescription paper requirement does NOT apply to prescriptions transmitted by...
- Phone.
- Fax.
- E-prescription.

For prescription paper to fulfill the tamper-resistant requirement, the paper must contain each of the following three (3) security features:
- At least one (1) feature to prevent unauthorized copying.
    - EXAMPLE: The word "VOID" or "ILLEGAL" appearing in the background when photocopied.
- At least one (1) feature to prevent erasure or modification of information written by the prescriber.
    - EXAMPLE: Checkboxes for quantities/refill authorizations or background ink that shows erasures.
- At least one (1) feature to prevent the use of counterfeit prescription forms.
    - EXAMPLE: Serial numbers or logos printed on the prescription paper.

If any of the required security features are not present on the prescription paper, the pharmacy may obtain verbal confirmation of the order from the prescribing practitioner to satisfy the tamper-resistant requirement.

LAW
PUBLIC LAW 110-28 Section 7002(b)
US Troop Readiness, Veterans' Care, Katrina Recovery, and Iraq Accountability Appropriations Act 2007

GUIDANCE DOCUMENTS
Available at <https://www.cms.gov/medicare-medicaid-coordination/fraud-prevention/fraudabuseforprofs/trp.html>

FDA RECALLS

CLASS I RECALL
Use of (or exposure to) the recalled product will cause serious adverse health effects up to and including death.

CLASS II RECALL
Use of (or exposure to) the recalled product may cause temporary or medically reversible adverse health effects.

CLASS III RECALL
Use of the recalled product is unlikely to cause adverse health effects.

REVIEW QUESTION

What is the most serious class of FDA recall?
The class I recall.

NDC NUMBERS

A National Drug Code (NDC) number is an 11-digit number composed of three (3) parts. The first part identifies who manufactured the product, the second part identifies what the product is, and the third part typically identifies the size of the package or the quantity of dosage units contained in the package. The standard format of an NDC number is as follows:

$$12345-1234-12$$

First Segment (5 digits)
The first segment of an NDC number identifies the manufacturer of the product (e.g. 00093 is the 5-digit code for TEVA and 52544 is the 5-digit code for Watson Pharmaceuticals).

Second Segment (4 digits)
The middle segment of an NDC number identifies the product made by the manufacturer (e.g. 0913 is Watson Pharmaceutical's 4-digit code for Norco® 5/325 mg).

Third Segment (2 digits)
The last segment of an NDC number usually identifies the package size of the product (e.g. the NDC number for a 100-tablet bottle of Watson Pharmaceutical's Norco® 5/325 mg is 52544-0913-<u>01</u>; whereas, the NDC number for a 500-tablet bottle is 52544-0913-<u>05</u>).

Note: In most cases, a leading zero is omitted from the NDC number displayed on the label of the manufacturer's stock bottle. For instance, the 11-digit NDC 00093-0287-01 would typically be displayed in one of the following three formats:

0093-0287-01
00093-287-01
00093-0287-1

PHARMACY LAW
SIMPLIFIED

OVER-THE-COUNTER DRUG LABELS
WHY PHARMACIES SHOULD AVOID RE-PACKAGING OTC BULK BOTTLES

Over-the-counter (OTC) drugs have strict and extensive labeling requirements that are enforced by the FDA. For this reason, it is generally not a good idea for pharmacies to re-package the contents of bulk over-the-counter drug bottles into smaller containers for resale.

OUTLINE OF INFORMATION REQUIRED TO APPEAR ON AN OTC DRUG PACKAGE LABEL (21 CFR § 201.66)

- DRUG FACTS
    - Active Ingredient(s) and strength or concentration per dosage unit.
    - Purpose(s).
- USE(S)
- WARNING(S)
- DIRECTIONS
    - Specific instructions based on age, recommended dose, frequency of dosing and maximum daily dose.
- OTHER INFORMATION
    - Storage requirements.

- INACTIVE INGREDIENTS
    - List of ingredients that do not affect therapeutic action, such as flavoring agents, colorants, and preservatives.
- CONTACT INFORMATION
    - Name, location, and phone number of the manufacturer.
- **Per 21 CFR § 211.132, a statement regarding the integrity of the tamper-evident packaging, such as "Do not use if safety seal is broken or missing." ***

---

* The FDA requires tamper-evident packaging for most OTC medications. This requirement was established after the 1982 Chicago Tylenol® Murders, where someone laced Tylenol® capsules with cyanide and returned the bottles to the shelf killing seven people.

RESTRICTED DRUG PROGRAMS

As we know, medications have potential benefits (the intended therapeutic effect) and risks (side effects). Drugs that cause more harm than good typically do not reach the market, or, if they have already entered the market, are withdrawn once the harm is recognized (e.g. Vioxx®). Some medications are capable of causing great harm and yet provide tremendous benefit for certain patients. This is where restricted drug programs come into play. Pursuant to the FDA Amendments Act of 2007, the FDA can require manufacturers to comply with programs that help manage the risks associated with the use of certain drugs. These programs are also referred to as "Risk Evaluation and Mitigation Strategies" (REMS). Over 100 drugs are associated with a REMS program. The most well-known REMS programs are iPLEDGE™, THALOMID REMS™, T.I.P.S., and Clozaril® National Registry. In this section of the study guide, we review the basic elements of each of these four programs.

iPLEDGE™
Isotretinoin is effective in the treatment of severe acne; however, the use of isotretinoin during pregnancy is associated with severe birth defects. Among other requirements, iPLEDGE™ primarily mitigates this risk by...

1) Ensuring that patients who begin isotretinoin therapy are not pregnant.
2) Preventing pregnancy in patients who receive isotretinoin.

OTHER IMPORTANT POINTS:
- ✓ Isotretinoin prescriptions are limited to a 30-day supply.
- ✓ Isotretinoin brand name formulations include Absorbica®, Accutane®, Amnesteem®, Claravis®, Myorisan®, Sotret®, and Zenatane®.

THALOMID REMS™ (formerly known as S.T.E.P.S.®)
Thalomid® (thalidomide) is effective in the treatment of multiple myeloma and erythema nodosum leprosum; however, the use of thalidomide during pregnancy is associated with severe birth defects (e.g. "The Thalidomide Tragedy"). Among other requirements, THALOMID REMS™ primarily mitigates this risk by...

1) Ensuring that patients who begin thalidomide therapy are not pregnant.
2) Preventing pregnancy in patients who receive thalidomide.

OTHER IMPORTANT POINTS:
- ✓ Thalidomide prescriptions are limited to a 28-day supply with no refills or telephone prescriptions.
- ✓ The THALOMID REMS™ program was previously known as S.T.E.P.S.® (System for Thalidomide Education and Prescribing Safety).

T.I.P.S.
T.I.P.S. stands for "Tikosyn® In Pharmacy System." Tikosyn® (dofetilide) is used to induce and maintain normal cardiac sinus rhythm in highly symptomatic patients with atrial fibrillation or atrial flutter; however, the use of dofetilide is associated with potentially fatal ventricular arrhythmias, especially in patients who are starting or re-starting the drug. T.I.P.S. mitigates this risk by...

1) Communicating the risk of cardiac arrhythmias associated with Tikosyn® (dofetilide).
2) Requiring patients who receive Tikosyn® (dofetilide) to be admitted to a facility for medical monitoring for at least three (3) days when starting or re-starting therapy.

Clozaril® National Registry

Clozaril® (clozapine) is effective in the treatment of various psychiatric disorders (e.g. schizophrenia, bipolar disorder); however, the use of clozapine is associated with the potentially fatal agranulocytosis (suppression of white blood cell production). Clozaril® National Registry mitigates this risk by…

1) Requiring WBC count to be recorded in the Clozaril® National Registry on a weekly basis for the first 6 months of therapy and then periodically thereafter.
2) Limiting the amount of the drug pharmacies can dispense to a quantity sufficient only to treat the patient until their next scheduled lab work (e.g. a 7-day supply every week for the first 6 months of therapy).

Note: Some people refer to this REMS program as the "No Blood, No Drug Program."

EACH REMS PROGRAM IS UNIQUE

Some REMS programs are so simple that you might not even realize they exist. A great example is Dulera® (mometasone/formoterol), for which the the REMS program imposes only one requirement – the manufacturer must communicate to healthcare providers the increased risk of asthma-related death associated with the use of long-acting beta agonists (such as the formoterol found in Dulera®).

OTHER IMPORTANT POINTS REGARDING REMS PROGRAMS

✓ Manufacturers may implement a REMS program for a drug in the absence of an FDA requirement to do so.

✓ The consequence for a manufacturer that fails to comply with a REMS program is a fine of at least $250,000 per incident.

LONG-TERM CARE FACILITY PHARMACY SERVICES

42 CFR § 483.60

Long-term care facilities must provide (or obtain from a provider pharmacy) routine and emergency drugs and biologicals for residents.

All drugs must be stored in locked, temperature-controlled compartments. Only authorized personnel can have access to the keys.

Schedule II controlled substances and other drugs of abuse must be stored in separately locked, permanently affixed compartments, unless the facility stores a small quantity of controlled substances in single unit package drug distribution systems and missing doses can be detected readily.

Long-term care facilities must employ (or obtain from a provider pharmacy) a pharmacist for consultation, recordkeeping, and to provide monthly drug regimen reviews for each resident.

A PHARMACIST MUST PROVIDE MONTHLY DRUG REGIMEN REVIEWS FOR EACH RESIDENT OF A LONG-TERM CARE FACILITY.

The pharmacist must report any irregularities to the physician and the facility's director of nursing, and these reports "must be acted upon."
⇧
At minimum, the pharmacist's recommendations must be acknowledged.

THE END

PHARMACY LAW
SIMPLIFIED

Copyright © 2016 by David Heckman
All rights reserved. This content is protected by copyright. The content of this book cannot be reproduced in any form, including mechanical or electronic reproduction, without the express written permission of the author.

NOTES

NOTES

NOTES

NOTES

Made in the USA
Columbia, SC
05 July 2018